Chinatown Jeet Kune Do

VOLUME 2

TRAINING METHODS OF BRUCE LEE'S MARTIAL ART

Tim Tackett

Chinatown Jeet Kune Do
VOLUME 2

TRAINING METHODS OF BRUCE LEE'S MARTIAL ART

Tim Tackett

Edited by Sarah Dzida, Wendy Levine and Oliver Gettell

Graphic Design by John Bodine

Photography by Tom Sanders

Models: Tim Tackett Jr., Dennis Blue, Jeremy Lynch,
Vince Raimondi and Patrick Cunningham

Printed in South Korea
Library of Congress Catalog Number: 2010926558
ISBN 10: 0-89750-189-6
ISBN 13: 978-0-89750-189-7

First Printing 2010

BLACK BELT BOOKS
A Division of **OHARA PUBLICATIONS, INC.**
World Leader in Martial Arts Publications

Dedications and Acknowledgments

I would like to dedicate this book to our son, Tim Tackett Jr.
May you rest in peace.
Love,
Mom & Dad

I also want to thank the following Wednesday Night Group instructors who posed for the photos in the book.

- Tim Tackett Jr.
- Dennis Blue
- Jeremy Lynch
- Vince Raimondi
- Patrick Cunningham

About the Author

In 1962, Tim Tackett's martial arts training began when the U.S. Air Force sent him and his family to Taipei, Taiwan. While there, Tackett trained in kung fu. When he returned with his family to California a few years later, Tackett opened a kung fu school. However, he was surprised to discover that he was one of the few non-Chinese kung fu teachers in America.

Tackett first saw Bruce Lee in 1967 at Ed Parker's International Karate Tournament. He decided then and there to study *jeet kune do*. Unfortunately, Tackett wasn't able to begin JKD training until after Lee's Chinatown school had officially closed. To fill the void, Dan Inosanto ran classes from the gym in his backyard. When Tackett joined the backyard class in 1971, there were only about 10 students in the class. Today, those students make up the who's who of jeet kune do, such as Bob Bremer, Peter Jacobs, Dan Lee, Richard Bustillo, Herb Jackson, Jerry Poteet and Tony Luna.

Today, Tackett is considered one of the leading authorities on jeet kune do. In addition to numerous magazine articles, Tackett is also the coauthor of *Chinatown Jeet Kune Do: Essential Elements of Bruce Lee's Martial Art* with original Bruce Lee student Bob Bremer, as well as a companion DVD.

About the Wednesday Night Group

After training under Dan Inosanto for four years, Tim Tackett asked whether he could share what he had learned from Inosanto with other people. By this time, Tackett was finding it harder to teach kung fu because he thought *jeet kune do* was much more efficient. When Inosanto told him that he could teach jeet kune do, but not to the general public, Tackett closed his school and started teaching a group in his garage every Wednesday night. He kept the class small and charged nothing for the lessons. This group became and is still called the Wednesday Night Group.

In the 1980s, Bob Bremer began attending the Wednesday Night Group, and what he shared was illuminating. Because of his private lessons with Bruce Lee, Bremer was able to go into great detail about how to make a technique work and how to strike at the correct range. Bremer also went into detail about certain principles, like the water hose, the whip and the hammer. In regards to the hammer principle, he taught the group how Lee used it as a means to strike with nonintention. Bremer also shared how Lee explained to him that the best way to win a fight was to simply reach over and knock an opponent out, to get rid of passive defensive moves and intercept an opponent's attack with enough power to immediately end the fight. Because of Bremer's participation, the Wednesday Night Group threw away inefficient techniques.

This instruction also helped Tackett notice that Lee had taught different things to different people. For example, Bremer was a big guy whose natural inclination was to crash the line and blast his opponent, and Lee accommodated that inclination in their private lessons. In contrast, Lee taught people with smaller builds, like Ted Wong, to rely on footwork to be elusive. And while both approaches are valuable, Bremer and Tackett understood that most JKD stylists retained what naturally worked best for them, which is the way Lee wanted JKD practitioners to learn. This method tends to benefit students more than a set curriculum, but it can be difficult for teachers because they are naturally inclined to fight a certain way, meaning they may not be aware that their style isn't necessarily the best for everyone. The Wednesday Night Group eventually came to believe that JKD practitioners should not be clones of their teachers. Instead, the student, while adhering to the basic principles of jeet kune do set by Bruce Lee, should still try to attain a unique expression of the art.

In the 1990s, Jim Sewell, another former Chinatown student, joined the Wednesday Night Group, bringing the same no-nonsense approach to fighting as Bremer had. Today, Sewell, Bremer and Tackett run the group together with the same basic approach to teaching, which is that all techniques must work against a skilled fighter. Of course, many techniques will work against an unskilled fighter, but the question is whether they will work against a seasoned street fighter, a skilled boxer, a classically trained Thai fighter, an experienced grappler or a JKD practitioner. If a technique doesn't work against any of those opponents, why bother learning it?

If you are interested in learning more about the Wednesday Night Group or contacting one of the instructors in this book, please visit www.jkdwednite.com.

Table of Contents

Introduction

All *jeet kune do* teachers have probably encountered the type of student who sees a technique and says, "Oh! I already know that." However, it soon becomes clear that the student recognizes rather than knows how to properly execute it. This is an important distinction because a JKD practitioner needs to understand a technique and all its dimensions. He must know why and when it needs to be executed. He needs to be able to react correctly to whatever situation he faces. He also needs to know which tool in his arsenal is the best to use at that moment. He may recognize what the correct distance and range is to fight his opponent, but that doesn't signify whether he knows how to properly maintain it. Or, to borrow from Bruce Lee, the skilled JKD practitioner knows that he must punch when he has to punch and kick when he has to kick—without a second thought.

A mentality like that is why intercepting and offensive tools, like the straight lead punch, are key to jeet kune do. It is the optimum defense to stop an attacker in his tracks, but a good JKD practitioner knows that it's not always the go-to technique. There are other facets to a fight. Sometimes you may need to use distance or footwork to retreat before you can enact an appropriate response. Sometimes you find yourself on the ground in a clinch. You may even find that you're facing an attacker with a weapon. In the end, no one technique can keep you safe in all situations. Instead, what you can do is approach self-defense from the following three angles:

- Hone the tools you have to be as effective as you can make them.
- Train as realistically as possible.
- Learn to sidestep trouble and/or never seek it.

For martial artists to achieve these angles, physical conditioning is usually a key component. However, plyometrics, weight training and other fitness exercises are not the focus of this book. The main goal of *Chinatown Jeet Kune Do Volume 2* is to take particular techniques, like the straight lead punch, and give you suggested methods on how to improve their efficiency.

Chinatown Jeet Kune Do Volume 2 mainly focuses on the first and second angles—honing your tools and training realistically for you. It is also meant to be a companion to the first *Chinatown Jeet Kune Do*, which is coauthored by Bruce Lee student Bob Bremer. *Chinatown Jeet Kune Do* explains the fundamentals. This book, Volume 2, will show you how to hone those fundamentals into proficient tools. Volume 1 details and illustrates, while Volume 2 delves deeper, trains and prepares you to apply those techniques and tools with enough force to get the job done in a combative situation. For clarity's sake,

Volume 2 is organized similarly to Volume 1. The chapters are in the same order and deal with the same subject matter to make cross-referencing easier. The only organizational difference is that Volume 1's Chapter 8 (Specialized Tools), is scattered throughout this book. Also, the final two chapters in this volume do not refer back to the original *Chinatown Jeet Kune Do*.

The drills and tools found in this book have come from a variety of resources over the years—my JKD teachers Dan Inosanto and Bob Bremer; the Wednesday Night Group's senior JKD instructors; other original Bruce Lee students like Dan Lee; and other JKD teachers, instructors and students. A few of the drills have even been adapted from other martial arts like *savate* and Thai boxing. Often, JKD practitioners invent because of the need to alter a technique's effectiveness based on an individual's ability. Many times, I've had to create a particular drill to help a student achieve correct timing or distance. It's like prescribing a particular medicine for a particular disease. After all, that's what Bruce Lee would do.

That is why this book is also meant to be no more than a guide to your training. Don't hesitate to reject what doesn't work for you. You may find that one drill works well for a while before you find another that does the same job or does it even better. Or you may find that familiar drills need to be revisited. No matter what, remember that study, application, versatility and change are good things for the JKD practitioner. I also encourage you to look beyond this book and apply what you've learned from other forums here. In fact, I also hope this book will give readers ideas on how to create their own drills.

Otherwise, there are a lot of drills in this book. For example, there are about 20 different drills for the straight lead punch alone. But all drills, no matter the technique, focus on important fighter attributes. Those attributes are:

- **Accuracy.** To make any punch or kick effective, you need to make sure that it will land at the precise spot where it will do the most damage. A football quarterback may work on the accuracy of his pass by throwing a football through a tire, while the martial artist can do the same thing by hitting or kicking a focus glove. The wobbly-glove drill in Chapter 3 is a good example of a drill that was designed primarily to work on the accuracy of a straight lead punch. (See page 42.)

- **Awareness.** Being able to react properly and with the correct response to a threat may have to be adjusted according to your environment. Awareness may also give you the ability to avoid a dangerous situation, which could be as simple as walking across the street to avoid a suspicious individual. Awareness is also an important component in seeing your opponent's preparation so you can respond quickly to his attack. The hammer principle is a good example of an awareness drill. Learn more about the hammer principle on pages 153-156 of Volume 1.

- **Balance.** If you throw a punch and end up off-balance, you leave yourself vulnerable to a counterattack. A balanced stance is key to moving in any direction and being able to reach a target as quickly as possible in any situation. When doing the drills in this book, try to maintain your equilibrium before, during and after a movement or technique.

- **Choice.** Choice is simply being able to select the appropriate tool to get the job done. It may be something as simple as a stop-kick to your opponent's knee when he punches. It may be more complex, like feinting to draw a response from an opponent and then following up with the correct choice of attack to an open line. Choice also means choosing the right response to a particular stimulus. There are many drills in this book that will address this aspect of training.

- **Power.** How can you effectively stop-hit an opponent if you do not have enough power to actually stop him? I've seen too many people hit focus gloves and other targets with great accuracy and balance but not enough power to stop a determined opponent. Because of this, JKD practitioners of the Wednesday Night Group and I spend a lot of our time working on getting maximum power into our tools. Most of the drills we practice for that are included in this book.

- **Range.** This important component refers to the distance you maintain in relation to your opponent. It also refers to keeping the proper distance from your opponent so you can defend and attack. Suppose, for instance, that your opponent is at close range, inside your fighting measure. Remember that the fighting measure is the ideal range to be from your opponent because he needs to take a step forward to be able to touch you. If he's too close, then you probably have little time to consider your best response. There are many drills in this book that work on maintaining the proper range and giving each tool optimum power at different ranges. In addition, sometimes JKD schools discuss the four ranges of combat: kicking, striking, trapping and grappling. At the Wednesday Night Group, we divide range into long, medium and close because these categories more accurately reflect the ranges you can kick, strike, trap and grapple in. For example, a hand tool like the straight lead punch may be best suited at medium range, while a shovel hook seems better suited at close range. Try to be aware of which range is being utilized in each exercise and drill in this book. Can you adapt it to another range, or is it best used at that range only?

- **Reaction.** You can have all the accuracy, power and balance in the world, but they won't do you any good if you can't react with the right timing to a situation. Many drills in this book deal with the proper reaction and timing for a particular stimulus.

- **Relaxation.** When you've been an instructor for as long as I have, you notice that students hold themselves back when they work on improving their striking power. For example, they might tighten a flexor muscle (like the biceps) when punching, which prevents them from using an extensor muscle (like the triceps) efficiently. They're tense and not relaxed, which isolates their power to one muscle; they don't fire with the whole group. Drills like those in Chapter 3 focus on learning how to punch while relaxed. Relaxation also refers to a fighter's mental state. When you're "in the zone," you are able to react properly to a situation.

- **Speed.** Speed is a complicated subject that encompasses more than moving from point A to point B. It consists of various components—perception, mentality, initiation, performance, alteration, sensitivity—and you need to train in all of them. Various drills in this book, like the raised-finger drill in Chapter 3, will help you develop faster initiation and reaction times. To learn more about speed, see the other aspects on page 14.

- **Timing.** Being able to time your attack or your opponent's attack is crucial to a successful attack or counterattack. There are many drills in this book that can help you achieve proper timing.

When working on the drills in this book, come back to this list again and again to see if you really understand the objective of the drill. Otherwise, I recommend that you approach each drill and evaluate its value as it pertains to your training. The importance of training is that you take what drills you have at hand and work on improving your performance every day. Without time and effort, there won't be much improvement. And in the end, your training should not be a chore or something you dread. Instead, it should be as enjoyable as possible. Just try to be a little better today than you were yesterday. You may find in your training that you hit a wall and can't seem to get better at a certain technique. This happens to everybody, but if you keep trying, you will break through that wall.

I wish you luck! And I hope this book helps you achieve a satisfactory level of success.

Other Aspects of Speed

Perceptual speed. Perceptual speed is the ability to see an opening for you to attack, or to see an attack coming and be able to counter it.

Mental speed. Mental speed is the ability to make the right choice about what to do in a particular situation. Should it be fight or flight? It's the ability to make the right choice at a moment's notice and then act on that choice.

Alteration speed. Alteration speed is the ability to change attacks in midstream. It's the ability to start a technique by punching on one line of attack and then change to another line. This may happen if you see that the first line is closed while another is opening up. All progressive indirect attacks in this book are based on being able to see a line opening (perceptual speed) and then being able to switch to another line of attack (alteration speed).

Initiation speed. Initiation speed is being in the right position to efficiently initiate an attack. Most JKD practitioners find it easier to start a punch from a fighting stance than a natural stance, such as having their hands in their pockets. Since you can't always be in a fighting stance, you must be able to hit from wherever your hands happen to be. There are some drills in Chapter 1 that deal with this subject.

Movement speed. Movement speed is how long it takes you to execute a technique, to move from point A to point B.

Performance speed. Performance speed is the speed of a technique from initiation to recovery. This differs from movement speed because it includes the time taken to get back to where you started.

Recovery speed. Recovery speed is how long it takes you to return to your starting position. Some of the drills in this book will show you that the more penetration in a particular punch, the slower your recovery will be. It will be even slower if you are off-balance when you strike.

Combination speed. Combination speed is the ability to hit and kick in combination with maximum speed while still having maximum power. When you work on any attack by combination in the book, make sure that you do not sacrifice power for speed or vice versa.

A Note to Readers on JKD Training

To help you achieve proficiency, *Chinatown Jeet Kune Do Volume 2* consists of drills designed to improve different technical, physical, mental and conceptual attributes that are necessary to efficiently attack and defend yourself. Many of the drills in this book are applicable to other drills, but that does not mean they are progressive. Some are basic drills and others are more advanced, but you should feel free to explore the material as though it were presented as a buffet rather than a four-course meal. Dive in at any point.

As you do each drill or training method, try to understand just what it is trying to accomplish. Does it work for you? Does it achieve its intended purpose?

However, there are general and overarching JKD themes that apply to all drills. Some of them were discussed in the Introduction, but they are important enough to restate here. They are:

- **Placing the strong side forward**. A primary JKD principle is to intercept and attack your opponent with the strong hand and foot leading. But you should also devote some time to training the other side. How much time you devote to either is up you.
- **Economy of motion**. JKD hand and kicking tools are meant to get you from point A to point B in the most efficient way possible.
- **Economy**. A tight attack and defense helps you achieve economy of motion, as well as many of the other concepts in this list, and vice versa. This idea of fighting economy helps you attack at a moment's notice while leaving no holes in your defense for an opponent to exploit.
- **Maintaining the fighting measure.** Keep your opponent at a position that is advantageous for you by trying to keep the fighting measure. In doing so, the attacker must step forward to touch you, which means he will telegraph his move with his step forward.
- **Using broken rhythm.** Break an opponent's attacking rhythm by intercepting him on half-beats.
- **Keeping it simple.** In *jeet kune do*, practitioners strive to execute a technique in the fewest moves and quickest time possible. Bruce Lee stressed simplicity and efficiency in his teachings and writings. He believed that many of the classical martial arts consisted of too many complex and flowery techniques.
- **Nontelegraphic movement.** You should consistently train to hide any attack preparation. Your movements should not clue your opponent in as to your intent.
- **Efficiency.** Use the least amount of effort to accomplish your objective. This obviously ties into economy, economy of motion and many other characteristics on this list.

- **Balance in motion.** JKD practitioners rely on speed, timing and distance. You want to remain balanced no matter your position so you are always ready to attack and defend.
- **Recovery.** Immediate recovery after any technique allows you to renew your offense or be able to return to the fighting measure quickly.
- **Relaxation.** Tension impedes movement and power. It isn't required to achieve an efficient and effective technique.
- **Awareness.** To effectively fight, you must be fully aware of your combative environment at all times.
- **Adaptability.** Make the necessary adjustments to prevail in a fight by instantly adjusting your tactics to changing circumstances. Some of the drills in this book will require that you do so.
- **Footwork.** Footwork controls the distance to defend or attack, as well as the fighting measure. You need to be able to move in any direction in relation to your opponent. Practice your footwork so you will always be in position to attack and/or defend in the most efficient and safe manner possible.

Be aware of these technical concepts when practicing a particular drill in this book (or any other JKD book or DVD) because they are interconnected. You can't focus on only one. For example, you may have a fast, powerful punch, but it will be of little use if you telegraph it, don't make contact with your intended target or leave holes in your defense. It's also important that your training partner be aware of all these concepts too. You need him to help you modify your training. He'll let you know things, like if you're off-balance or slow at recovery. This is why you should both refer back to this list whenever necessary.

Chapter 1
STANCES

At the Wednesday Night Group, we tend to go through a process when training a technique. Consider a technique like the basic straight lead punch: We practice transitioning from the natural stance to the fighting stance. From there, we practice the punch with basic footwork—stepping forward, stepping backward, curving right or left, etc. We do this in order to learn which one works best with it and how to control and strike with the technique from any distance. We then learn how to defend against the tool, attack with it and counterattack with it. This is followed by a discussion on tactics and strategy. The process is finalized with sparring, in which we work on getting rid of preparation, practicing natural follow-ups, etc. But this whole process, and really the whole training process, begins with stance.

There are two JKD stances: the natural stance and the fighting stance. For the most part, the drills in this chapter discuss how to transition from a natural to a fighting stance. The fighting stance in *jeet kune do* obviously implies a combat-ready position. The natural stance is meant to appear nonthreatening.

Why is it important to appear nonthreatening when confronted with a possible threat? There are two main reasons:

- **It telegraphs your intention to your opponent.** Think about it: How many people have gotten into sticky situations because they immediately jumped into a fighting stance? It's to your advantage for your attacker to think that you aren't a threat. In fact, it's even better if you never have to transition into a fighting stance. In the Wednesday Night Group, we actually train on how to respond to verbal assaults in a nonthreatening manner. It's interesting that more than one student has been able to defuse a tense "What are you looking at?" situation with a smile and the answer, "I was wondering where you got that shirt."

- **We live in a litigious society.** It's not uncommon for the intended victim in a street confrontation to be sued by an attacker whom he injured in self-defense. In fact, the consequences of an attack could fall on the victim's shoulders even more so if he begins in a fighting stance. Potential witnesses may remember you as the victim, but they'll also remember that you showed aggression, which makes you legally culpable. And even if you are shown to be right, you may spend time in jail. Wednesday Night Group instructor Jim Sewell had a friend who got into an argument with a drunken man at a bar. They took the argument outside, and the drunken man threw a punch, which missed. Jim's friend hit back, and the drunken man fell, hit his head on the ground and died later at the hospital. Jim's friend was arrested, charged and convicted of manslaughter. He was given six years in prison. So, avoid a street confrontation at all costs!

Also note that in any natural stance, you want to keep almost all of your weight on the rear leg. This will keep the front leg free for kicking. It also maintains your mobility because you'll be able to quickly push off in any and all directions. At the same time, you want to have your strong hand and foot forward so you can stop-hit or stop-kick with maximum power.

Transitioning From Natural Stances to Fighting Stances

In this drill, you'll practice going from a natural stance to a fighting stance. Face your training partner in a natural stance. Your training partner then attacks you with various hand and kicking tools, and you practice intercepting them from the natural stance. In the process of doing so, you will recover into a fighting stance and work on such important attributes as range, speed, accuracy lack of preparation. Note: Your training partner will start at the fighting measure, which is important to learn to maintain in training. It is the optimal distance and is a point students often forget! Learn more about proper distance on page 24 of Volume 1.

Pleading Stance

A

B

A: Patrick Cunningham (left) acts aggressively toward Vince Raimondi (right). Raimondi is in a natural "pleading" stance with his hands up. However, Raimondi's strong hand and foot are forward and the majority of his weight is on his rear leg, making him ready to attack at a moment's notice if necessary.

B: When Cunningham tries to grab Raimondi, Raimondi intercepts the attack with a finger jab. Note: The finger jab can do serious damage and should only be used in the direst of circumstances. The Wednesday Night Group usually teaches students to only use the finger jab with the pleading stance because you verbally tell the attacker not to come closer. If he continues to do so, the natural stance helps it make it look like the attacker accidentally ran into the student's fingers.

Casual Stance

A

A: Raimondi casually stands in a thoughtful position. However, what his attacker Cunningham does not realize is that this puts him in a natural offensive position.

B

B: When Cunningham steps forward to strike Raimondi with his left hand, Raimondi intercepts by throwing a backhand chop to Cunningham's neck/jaw. When stepping forward, Raimondi moves slightly to the left with his lead foot, which puts him inside of Cunningham's attack.

Hands-on-Hips Stance

A: Raimondi faces attacker Cunningham with his hands on his hips. As in the other stances, his strong hand and foot are forward.

B: When Cunningham executes a punch, Raimondi parries and hook-kicks to Cunningham's groin.

Hands-Low Stance

A: Raimondi's hands are low in this stance, leaving the entire top half of his body open to attack. However, Cunningham doesn't realize that Raimondi is doing this purposely. Raimondi plans to draw Cunningham into executing a high attack. Because Raimondi is prepared for the high attack, he will be able to counter it effectively.

B: Cunningham steps forward to punch Raimondi's head, but Raimondi avoids the hit by pushing off with his right foot to step to the side with his left leg. He simultaneously parries the punch with his left hand while using his right hand to execute a strike at Cunningham's face.

Fighting-Stance Transition When Pushed From Behind

A: Cunningham (right) prepares to attack Raimondi (left) who is unaware of his approach. In the real world, it's common to be surprised by an attacker from behind, so this is an excellent training scenario.

B: Raimondi doesn't tense up at the surprise attack. Instead, he goes with the flow.

C: Raimondi steps out with his left foot and throws a finger slice at Cunningham's eye. Note: The finger slice can do serious damage to an opponent and should only be used in the direst of situations, such as when you need to incapacitate an opponent as quickly as possible. Learn more about the finger slice on page 55 of Volume 1.

The Circle Practice Group Exercise

This group exercise also trains you on transitioning from a natural to a fighting stance. You will need four or more training partners to complete this practice. Designate one as the trainer. To do the drill: Have your training partners stand in a circle around you at the fighting measure or a little bit farther. You stand in the center in a natural stance with your eyes closed. The trainer points to one of the other training partners. The appointed training partner makes a sound by yelling or clapping his hands. The defender, you, must then face whoever made the sound in a fighting stance. It doesn't matter what stance the people in the circle are standing in.

It's also easy to modify the drill. For example, stand in the center of your circled training partners with your eyes open. The training partners take turns taking a step forward, or bridging the gap, and executing a throw, punch or kick. The defender, which is you, needs to counter by facing the opponent, transitioning out of the natural stance to intercept the attack, and then recovering in a fighting stance.

Correct Hand Position Exercise

When at a long distance from your opponent, such as beyond the fighting measure, it is perfectly all right to keep your hands in a low position. This is because the opponent will have to move forward to hit you with a hand attack to the face. In fact, a hands-low stance can sometimes give you better balance when moving at long range. However, you want to make sure your hands can assume the proper position—into an airtight upper-body and head defense—when you move from a long range and into the fighting measure.

Note that the fighting measure will be different every time you train with a different person because of the individual's different arm and leg length. When practicing this drill, it's possible to do it with one opponent stationary, both moving, or one opponent stationary while the other moves in and out of the fighting measure.

Fighting Measure Exercise

A

B

A: JKD practitioners Raimondi and Cunningham train at a distance so their hands are low.

B: Cunningham moves forward slowly and into his fighting measure. Raimondi doesn't move. When both feel they are approaching the fighting measure, they move their hands into the proper combat-ready position. Raimondi and Cunningham could also practice this drill by both moving.

C

C: At close range, their hands are up to parry a hand attack.

From here, be creative and use these example drills as a springboard to come up with many more of your own. You may find that with a little tweaking, you can change a drill for stance into a drill for another technique. You may also want to mix up other JKD elements, like range, in the drill. Don't feel bound by this book. My experience has taught me that practitioners have a good reason to add, change or remove a drill in almost every class.

Chapter 2
FOOTWORK

Bruce Lee believed that footwork was the essence of fighting because it helps you control the distance between you and your opponent. Proper footwork is also crucial to bridging the gap to attack effectively, or it can be used to create an opportunity to force your opponent off-balance. However, many students and practitioners don't often focus enough energy on footwork during training, which can be detrimental in a real-life situation.

The drills in this chapter aren't unique to the Wednesday Night Group. Instead, they are effective drills used by many other JKD groups around the world. You can practice these drills alone or with a partner. Here are some footwork components you should keep in mind when tweaking footwork drills:

- **Distance.** Vary it. Don't always begin and end each drill at the same distance. Practice them from all ranges too—long, medium and close.
- **Rhythm.** Vary it. Attack, defend and counterattack with different rhythm. Learn more about rhythm on pages 110-112 of Volume 1.

Combine and mix your variations with distance and rhythm when practicing. In addition, when practicing a hand or kicking tool, make sure that you train executing it with footwork, rhythm and distance. For example, practice throwing a straight lead punch with the following:

- **A lead step.** This movement is when you just step forward with the lead foot; the rear stays in place. It is used when you don't have very much distance to travel to connect with a punch. Learn more about the lead step on page 40 of Volume 1.
- **One or multiple push-steps.** These steps are useful when you are close enough to your opponent to consider an attack but too far out to take a lead step in. Learn more about push-steps on page 118 of Volume 1.
- **Curved right or left with a straight lead punch.** To perform a curved punch, you use footwork to step forward and to the left or right. This creates the strike's arced trajectory. Learn more about curved punches on pages 91-92 of Volume 1.
- **Step-out.** You usually use a step-out left when in a right lead. When your opponent attempts to punch, you slip inside the hit while countering with a hit of your own. It's reversed if you are in a left lead. Learn more about step-outs on pages 93-94 of Volume 1.
- **Step-back straight lead punch.** If you are too close to your opponent to use the

straight lead effectively, you can get the proper distance by stepping back. You step back with your rear foot and push with your front foot while punching. Learn more about the step-back on pages 44-45 of Volume 1.

- **Steal a step.** You can steal a step with a hand attack by moving the rear foot further forward as you push forward with a hand attack. Learn more about stealing a step on pages 119-120 of Volume 1.
- **Do combination attacks.** Use attacks by combination with kicking and hand tools and appropriate footwork.

Of course, it's important to practice your hand and kicking tools with any footwork that is efficient for that particular technique. Trial and error in training will reveal what is best for you.

Maintaining the Fighting Measure (Mirror Drill)

The mirror drill is the basic footwork drill for learning how to keep the fighting measure. To do this drill, two JKD practitioners face each other. One is designated the defender while the other is designated the attacker. They stand at each other's fighting measure. The attacker will try to bridge the gap with footwork—such as a push-step or lead step— to close the distance between him and the defender. The defender will use footwork to maintain it. This reaction is also why the drill is known as the mirror drill: The defender and attacker mirror, or perform the same footwork, as one another to maintain their fighting measure. It's also possible for the attacker and defender to switch roles in this drill. When the attacker breaks the fighting measure, the defender maintains it. Then they switch roles without changing positions. The attacker is now the defender and must maintain his fighting measure.

Note that the attacker should vary both his distance and rhythm of attack. This means that it will be harder for the attacker to anticipate what the defender will do next. The drill should eventually become so practiced that a bystander would not be able to tell which person actually moves first, and that's probably the case for the two practitioners as well. Like Bruce Lee said, we should strive to learn to move like sound and echo.

The Mirror Drill

A: Vince Raimondi (left) and Patrick Cunningham (right) stand at the fighting measure.

B: When Cunningham push-steps forward, Raimondi push-steps back.

C, D, E, F: Raimondi and Cunningham continue the drill. They sidestep while trying to maintain the fighting measure.

G, H: Raimondi now quickly push-steps forward to break the fighting measure while Cunningham retreats. In this case, Cunningham has not retreated far enough, and Raimondi is in range to hit him with a straight lead punch.

Breaking the Fighting Measure (Shadow-Closing Drill)

The shadow-closing drill is similar to the mirror drill. The difference is that this time the designated attacker wants to keep the fighting measure broken. His goal is to bridge the gap to get as close to his partner as quickly as possible. His ultimate goal is to not let the designated defender escape. The student can do this with a push-step followed by stealing a step, as fast and as deep as he can, as long as the two do not touch. After doing this drill awhile, the trainer will then move in different directions while the student tries to keep the same distance. The trainer can move forward and back, left and right; he can circle, and he can stop and then move. Later the trainer can put on a set of focus gloves, and the student can practice the various punches as he bridges the gap while trying to keep the optimum punching distance.

The difference between this drill and the mirror drill concerns who moves first. In the mirror drill, the attacker moves first with the intention that his partner will maintain the fighting measure. In the shadow-closing drill, it is the opposite because you don't want to maintain the fighting measure but be the first to bridge the gap. In other words, you want to get into your partner's fighting measure and not let him get it back. The mirror drill is defensive, and the shadow-closing drill is offensive.

Maintaining and Breaking the Fighting Measure

There are two variations to this Western fencing-based drill. The first variation starts with two practitioners facing each other at a distance in a fighting stance. They extend their lead arms and adjust their stances until their fingertips touch. This gives the defender the distance that he wants to maintain and gives the attacker the distance that he needs to bridge. They drop their hands into a ready-stance position and begin the drill. Practitioner A push-steps forward twice while practitioner B maintains the fighting measure. Practitioner A could even try to steal a step when recovering after his first step. His goal is to execute a finger jab to practitioner B's forehead. While practitioner A is breaking the fighting measure, practitioner B is trying to maintain it. He uses footwork to keep enough distance between him and his partner to not get touched. The two switch roles after practitioner A's two steps.

Like the other drills discussed, this is an example of a cooperative drill. The attacking practitioner should vary his distance, rhythm and footwork, like stealing a step, so that the defending practitioner must learn to adjust to a different fighting measure.

The second variation of this drill is the non-cooperative version. It begins the same, but this time, the defending practitioner counterattacks as soon as the attacker has executed his finger jab. While the cooperative drill is to help the attacker learn how to move forward quickly, the non-cooperative drill teaches the one attacked to defend with a stop-hit.

In both drills, you should take no more than two steps each before switching roles. Go back and forth until you or your partner scores.

Experimenting With Footwork

Remember that footwork is the main element in making your attacks and defenses work in combat. So make sure that you know the purpose for each footwork or pattern movement you do. Is it to keep the fighting measure? Is it to defend against an attack by using distance? Is it to draw a second attack so you can counter it? Is it for a counterattack? If you are working by yourself, try to visualize an opponent. If you're working with a partner, make it as alive as possible.

Experimenting with footwork is another way to practice balance. The student moves by himself, practicing different footwork patterns while in an on-guard position. The trainer yells "stop." The student immediately halts. He should be balanced and still have his proper fighting stance. The following is also a decent group drill to do with a class.

Push-Step Forward

A, B: Vince Raimondi moves forward by pushing off with his left foot. He does it two or more times in a row, trying to increase his speed. He would push-step backward by pushing off with his front foot.

Slide Back to a Push-Step Forward (Solo Practice)

A, B, C. D, E: From a fighting stance, Raimondi slides his front foot back and follows up with a push-step as soon as his rear foot touches the ground. He pushes forward with his rear foot.

Slide Back to a Push-Step Forward (Partner Practice)

A, B, C: JKD practitioners use this combination to retreat against a kick and then move quickly back in with a hand counterattack.

Heel-and-Toe Sway

A: Patrick Cunningham (right) lead-steps forward while throwing a straight lead punch to Vince Raimondi's head.

B: Raimondi avoids the punch by dropping down on his rear foot and swaying back just enough.

C: He returns a straight lead to Cunningham's head as he transfers his weight to his front foot. With practice, Raimondi will be fast enough to hit Cunningham before he recovers his fighting stance or counterattacks. Learn more about the heel-and-toe sway on page 88 of Volume 1.

Rear Foot Step-Back

A, B, C: Raimondi (left) steps back with his rear foot so he is out of range of Cunningham's punch. This footwork has the same purpose as the heel-and-toe sway. However, while it is easier to execute, it is harder to break the attacker's rhythm because it takes more time to return a hit.

Slide-Up on Rear Foot to Straight Lead Punch

A, B: Raimondi bridges the gap for a punch by sliding his rear foot up.

C: He then pushes off with the same foot as he steps forward with a straight lead punch. This kind of footwork gives you a very fast and powerful way to bridge the gap.

Pendulum to Front Kick

A, B: Raimondi slides back with his front foot and keeps his weight on the front leg. This is the "pendulum."

C, D: He then slides back with his rear foot and kicks with his front leg. This pendulum footwork allows him to retreat against a kicking attack and then quickly counter with a kick.

Pivot

A

B

A, B: Use the pivot when your opponent attempts to circle you or move to the side. You pivot by sliding your rear foot in the direction you want to go while facing your opponent. Practice pivoting to face your opponent by sliding with your rear foot until you end up back where you started.

————⌒∿⌒————

These are just a few of the many possible footwork drills. Come up with as many as you find practical. For example, you could practice curving right followed by a lead step, or a push-step, a slide-step forward or back, etc. Be creative. Experiment with as many different combinations of footwork as possible. When training or creating your own drills, think about how an opponent would move or react. He can either move away from you, move toward you, attack, retreat, counter, etc. The opponent can vary his distance, rhythm and attacks, and when he drills footwork, so should you.

Chapter 3
HAND TOOLS

This chapter deals with different ways to practice the hand tools that are shown in detail in Volume I. If you have any specific questions on how to perform a particular punch, please refer to Chapter 3 in Volume 1.

There are many hand-tool drills in this book. There are about 20 different drills that incorporate the straight lead punch alone. But as I mentioned in the Introduction, many of these drills can be tailored to other hand tools. You may even find some are useful for working on various kicks. The important thing is to remember that while a drill is shown with a particular tool, it can be used or adapted for another technique or tool.

You also want to make sure that you understand the tactics and strategy for each hand tool—what is the best way to use it and when is the best time to implement it. This kind of understanding also includes being aware of what techniques and attacks will work on what types of opponents. This book deals with many examples, but you should look at any potential attack and think to yourself: While I'm doing this, what can my opponent do to me? Be aware of what you are offering a potential attacker because a skilled opponent will know how to take advantage of an opening. And what to do, where to do it, when to do it and whom to do that technique to are things that can only come from experience and a lot of practice working with different types of opponents.

Training Tips

Consider that the person who controls the drill by holding the equipment or setting the environment is the trainer, even if he is a less advanced student than the person who is practicing the drill. The person doing the exercise or drill is considered a student even if he has far more experience than the trainer. The trainer has the responsibility to watch for and point out errors to the student because even advanced practitioners develop bad habits over the years. Even a small error, like a slight but telegraphic preparation before a hit, can become exaggerated over time if it is not pointed out.

For example, the trainer should be aware of the errors that can occur in a straight lead punch. Those errors are illustrated in the sequences that follow, so the trainer needs a sharp eye to notice subtler ones. Note that they are exaggerated to show the worst-case scenario.

Dropping the Rear Arm

A: JKD practitioner Dennis Blue (right) drops his rear arm when hitting, which is bad because it exposes the left side of his head to attack. Instead, Blue should keep his rear arm near his chin so that his head is completely protected at all times.

Pulling the Rear Arm

A: Blue pulls his rear arm back, which also exposes the left side of his head. Sometimes martial artists punch this way because they believe it gives them greater power and follow-through with a punch. Whatever the reason, it is a bad habit. Instead, Blue should make sure that his hands are always near his chin so he can defend himself.

Dropping the Arm After a Hit

A: Like in the previous sequences, Blue exposes his head when he drops his attacking arm after a punch. Instead, he should snap his arm back into a ready fighting stance so he can renew his attack or make his defense airtight.

Opening the Centerline

A: Blue opens his centerline by moving his punching arm to the left after completing his hit. The centerline is the line that runs directly down the center of the body from the top of the head to the groin. By having your front arm at the center of your face and your elbow tucked in, you are in the best defensive position to defend the most vulnerable parts of your body. Learn more about posture on page 15 of Volume 1.

Pulling the Hand Before a Punch

A, B: Blue pulls his hand just before he punches. This is both a common problem and a dangerous habit because it telegraphs Blue's intent. If done in combat, this gives an opponent time to attack on preparation, meaning he intercepts. Learn more about attacking on preparation on page 80 of Volume 1.

Attacking Off-Balance

A

A: Blue puts too much weight on his front leg by raising his rear foot off the ground as he punches. This leaves him off-balance, which makes it easier for the trainer to counterattack. It also makes it much harder for Blue to recover for a follow-up punch or kick.

No matter how big or small the error, they all leave an opening for your opponent to exploit or leave you off-balance and unable to quickly recover your fighting stance. Many of these errors will show up in training other tools, and the trainer should watch carefully when drilling any tool with the student so that they can be corrected.

In addition to the above, most of the drills in this chapter are discussed with the student executing a strike from the right lead. This is because the right lead is the dominant hand for most practitioners, which makes it the more powerful hand tool to intercept attacks. However, you want to make sure to spend time with the opposite lead because it will not only make your weaker side stronger but also make you a more well-rounded fighter. After all, you never know when you might have to execute attacks, counterattacks or defenses with your weaker side.

To make the training feel as alive as possible, I recommend doing many of these drills with boxing or focus gloves. In fact, many of the drills in this chapter deal with one or more focus gloves. In addition, most of the drills can be set up for an exact number of variations, or they can be done in a series of rounds of various lengths. And many of the drills shown in Chapter 3 can be done with various kicking tools. For example, any of the distance drills can be done with kicks.

For safety, anytime you work with a partner and practice hitting a specific target on or near him, make sure you are at the proper distance. And go slowly at first because you do not want to injure him. Work up to full speed.

Finally, keep the following in mind while training in these drills:

- Most of them start at the fighting measure.
- Any drill that starts from the fighting measure will also mean that you will want to recover to it after a hit or punch.
- Make sure you vary the rhythm of your training. Do not go: "One, two, three, punch" every time you plan to make a hit.
- Most drills should start slow and then pick up speed as the student progresses.

Basic Focus Gloves for the Trainer

A: Tim Tackett Jr. demonstrates the proper focus-glove position for a straight lead punch, jab or straight rear punch.

B: Tim Tackett Jr. demonstrates the proper focus-glove position for a high-hook punch.

C: This is the proper position for the backfist.

D: This is the proper position for the low hook punch.

E: This is the proper position for the front or rear uppercut.

Training For Proper Distance

The power of the straight lead punch comes from the speed of the punch and the snap of the elbow at the end of it. When the punch is completely extended, it should have penetrated an optimum distance of two inches beyond the target. Sometimes you may be too close to the target, and sometimes you are too far away to achieve that penetration. If you are too far away, you can use footwork as you strike to gain the proper distance by moving closer. If you are too close, you may still achieve enough power, but only if you have worked on properly snapping your elbow through focus-glove training. And while it is easier to get power the farther the punch travels, you can develop the bad habit of pushing your hit instead of snapping it.

To snap your elbow, you need to keep your shoulders square. Try to snap it as much as possible to penetrate the glove by approximately two inches beyond the target. The focus glove will let you know if you've done it correctly. If you throw a proper snappy punch, the focus glove will make a loud popping sound. If the punch makes contact at the wrong distance, the sound will be more of a dull thud.

To practice striking at the right distance, throw straight lead punches with power at the trainer. The trainer will hold a focus glove. Start inside the fighting measure and close to the focus glove. At this distance, you are too close to get the proper penetration when executing a strike, so you will need to step back while hitting. If you push-step back too far, then you will need to add footwork to correct the distance. Continue your practice by moving closer and farther in relationship to the trainer. Vary what punches you use so that you learn which work best at what distance. The drill will also show you how you can use certain parts of your body to augment power. Learn more about distance on page 45 of Volume 1.

Power and Proper Distance

A: Because it's not always possible to fight at the fighting measure, Tim Tackett (right) practices at a closer distance. Even at close range, he punches with the proper snap without stepping back. He hits the focus glove with all the speed and snap he can generate. If he does it correctly, the glove will make a loud popping sound.

B: Having moved a little further back but still closer than the fighting measure, Tackett uses his shoulder to reach and hit his target with the proper penetration.

C: Moving back even farther, Tackett is now at the fighting measure. He uses torque to propel his punch across the distance. He achieves this by twisting his rear foot and hip. However, while this gives him maximum power, it also puts him slightly off-balance. It would have been better if he had taken a lead step before punching. (Remember the fighting measure is defined as that distance where either you or your opponent must take a step forward to make proper contact and still have balance.)

D: At the fighting measure, Tackett steps forward with his lead foot to hit with a straight lead punch. Note: When doing this footwork, make sure to push off your rear foot with as much velocity as possible.

E: When Tackett finds that he's too far away to use a lead step, he uses a push-step instead to cover more distance.

F, G: Tackett also practices throwing punches at a close distance. In this position, he needs to do a step-back punch. To execute it, he push-steps backward with his lead foot while punching. Tackett's punch should penetrate the target a split second before his rear foot lands. Note: The harder and faster he pushes back, the harder the punch will be. In addition, many JKD practitioners find a horizontal fist is the most comfortable with this punch, but experiment with the angles until you find what works best for you. Learn more about the step-back punch on pages 44-45 of Volume 1.

Learning to Relax

When punching, you don't want your arm to be tense, especially your biceps. Because the biceps is a flexor muscle that is used for any pulling motion, tensing it will only slow down the speed of your punch. Instead, you want to keep it relaxed for maximum speed and snap.

In this drill, the student will stand with his arms at his side. He will shake them vigorously to relax them. The student will then start to strike the focus glove a split second before he stops shaking his arms. Practice this drill with both left and right punches.

Shaking-Arms Drill

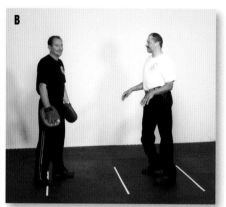

A: Dennis Blue stands as close to the focus glove as he can get and still hit it with only his shoulder and the snap of his elbow to get power.

B: Blue shakes his lead arm to keep it loose.

C: He executes a straight lead punch. To get proper penetration, he also extends his shoulder.

Power and Penetration (1-to-5 Drill)

Penetrating your target by two inches is the optimum level of power you want to achieve in a punch. However, it's important to learn greater control, and that is accomplished by learning how to penetrate a target with different power levels. The 1-to-5 drill will demonstrate the differences between striking a target by just touching the surface and penetrating the full two inches. The less penetration you have, the less power is in your strike. However, less power may be exactly what is necessary in a particular situation. Even in power there must be control. You may not always want to inflict maximum damage to an opponent. This is especially true in a friendly sparring situation in which you may want to only surface-punch the opponent's head. This drill will let the student experience different levels of power, which will help him deliver whatever the circumstances dictate.

The "1-to-5" in this drill refers to the different penetration levels that you will use to strike the focus glove. You should still execute each strike at full speed and power. The levels are:

- No. 1: Imagine an egg is inside the focus glove. At this level, you want to penetrate the glove just far enough to crack the shell but not smash it.
- No. 2: Penetrate the target only a half-inch. When you hit the target, you only penetrate half an inch into it.
- No. 3: Follow through with a 1-inch penetration.
- No. 4: Follow through with a 1½-inch penetration.
- No. 5: At this level, you penetrate the target the full two inches.

Practice striking from levels 1 to 5 and from 5 to 1. Once you have gotten the idea and can hit the target at all five levels of penetration at will, the trainer should then call out a distance, in any order. Once you have perfected this drill, you'll be able to deliver whatever power you feel the situation calls for. But remember to consider timing! The greater your penetration, the longer it will take for you to complete the attack and recover. Learn a similar drill on pages 112-113 of Volume 1.

Hip Action

Twisting your hip and using your whole body to punch is important in order to get full power in any punch. The drill below will help you get the idea of how to use your hip when punching. Because you do this drill standing on one leg, it also helps you work on balance.

The trainer holds the focus glove, and the student stands on one leg to punch. The trainer can just stand there while the student hits the focus glove in the beginning, but to make it more difficult, the trainer can move, making the student hop to get correct distance to punch. This adds a good aerobic element to the exercise. Here are four variations:

- Stand on right leg and punch with right arm.
- Stand on right leg and punch with left arm.
- Stand on left leg and punch with right arm.
- Stand on left leg and punch with left arm.
- You can do the above in timed rounds, and you can do each standing on the same leg or switching legs during each round.

One-Leg Drill

A: Jeremy Lynch stands on one leg.

B: He punches the focus glove. You can see the hip action when Lynch's hip goes forward when he punches.

Accuracy (Wobbly-Glove Drill)

To have an effective punch, you need to be accurate and hit your target exactly.

The wobbly-glove drill forces you to have an accurate punch. To do the drill, the trainer holds the glove while relaxing his hand. If the student does not hit the focus glove directly in the center, the glove will twist and the student's punch will slide off the glove. In the Wednesday Night Group, we usually do this exercise with the student in a stationary position. The student executes strikes from the fighting measure or beyond to include footwork practice in the drill.

Wobbly-Glove Drill

A: Dennis Blue (left) holds the focus glove in a very relaxed manner so that the glove will twist if Jeremy Lynch doesn't hit it in the exact center. Here Lynch is close enough to the glove to hit it without stepping forward.

B: Lynch strikes the glove, but since he does not hit it in the exact center, the glove twists. If he had hit it in the center, the glove would have moved straight back.

Making the Right Response

A reaction drill is a drill that trains a particular response for a particular stimulus. For example, by learning to maintain the fighting measure, you learn that your opponent must move forward to make contact with you. In knowing that, you can train for several responses. The opponent may pull his hand back when he moves forward to attack. That would be a signal for you to learn to take advantage of—respond with a counterattack. Any time you counterattack, you are responding to a certain stimulus.

There are endless reaction drills. In fact, you'll notice many other drills in this section are reaction drills. They can be done with almost any technique, and you'll notice there are many more reaction drills beyond this small section throughout the book.

Raised-Finger Drill:

A: Dennis Blue (left) holds a focus glove for Jeremy Lynch (right). Blue's other hand is held high in a fist.

B: He signals to Lynch by raising his index finger.

C: When Lynch sees the raised finger, he hits the focus glove with a straight lead punch. Note: This is one of the first reaction drills that students learn at the Wednesday Night Group.

Moving-Glove Drill With Telegraphing

A: As the trainer, Blue wants to move the focus glove if he sees any preparation on the part of the student, Lynch. Blue wants to start the drill inside the fighting measure so Lynch doesn't have to move forward to strike the focus glove.

B: Lynch telegraphs his punch by pulling his hand back before striking.

C: In seeing the preparation, Blue steps back so Lynch can no longer make contact. Once Lynch has gotten to the point where he has no preparation at a close distance, then he and Blue will train at the fighting measure. From there, Lynch will learn how to get rid of his preparation when taking a step forward.

Moving-Glove Drill Without Telegraphing

A: Lynch wants to move without any visible preparation. One drill to get rid of a student's preparation is to move the glove so he can't hit it. You want to move it if you see any preparation.

Dropping Your Weight

By dropping your weight as you punch, you can increase its power. This is sometimes called a "falling step."

When starting the drill, exaggerate your drop by hitting from a raised-leg position. It gives you the correct feel you should have when dropping weight into a punch. Start with your leg raised. Drop it to the ground, landing the punch a split second before the foot touches the floor. This enables the punch's power to follow through. To see the difference, try punching after dropping your weight. You'll notice a difference in how much power is generated.

Falling Step

A: Jeremy Lynch (right) faces a focus glove.

B: He raises his leg.

C: He drops his weight, making sure to make contact with the focus glove a split second before his raised leg hits the floor.

Stomp-Step With Toes

A: Jeremy Lynch is in a fighting stance facing trainer Dennis Blue.

B: Lynch lifts his toes.

C: Lynch stomps when he hits so his punch lands at the same time his foot hits the ground. While we don't recommend this all the time, sometimes you can get a little more power with a punch if you stomp with your front foot as you strike. Note: While you can get a little more power by stomping, it's not always recommended because it can be telegraphic. To prevent telegraphing, punch at the same time you lift your foot.

Stomp-Step With Heel

A: Lynch faces his trainer, Blue.

B: When Lynch goes to punch, he lifts his heel to stomp.

C: Lynch executes his punch so his heel lands at the same time his fist hits the glove. Note: It doesn't matter if you stomp by lifting your toes or heel. It's a matter of personal preference and power.

Punch After a Fake Kick

A: Lynch faces his trainer, Blue.

B: Lynch feints a kick before bridging the gap. This raises his leg, which will allow him to drop his weight into the punch.

C: Lynch drops his weight and punches the focus glove. He makes sure to make contact with the glove a split second before his foot touches the ground.

D: Lynch hits just before his foot touches the ground. Notice how the impact of the punch has slammed Blue's focus glove backwards.

Punch After a Real Kick

A: Lynch faces his trainer, Blue.

B: Lynch kicks with a front kick. Now he can drop his weight.

C: He drops his weight to gain more power when he punches the focus glove.

Punching at Different Angles

Punching while moving off the centerline and attacking at an angle rather than straight on is very important. This is because it is harder for your opponent to defend himself when you hit on an angle instead of straight on. When you are facing an opponent straight on, he is protecting the most vulnerable parts of his body, which lie along a straight line from his nose to his groin—the centerline. Dan Inosanto used to tell us backyard students that when an opponent is facing you with his fists covering his centerline, it's as if he has two guns pointed straight at you. By angling to the inside or outside of an attacker's centerline, you can more easily penetrate his defense.

It is also good to be able to angle away from your opponent's attack; doing so allows you to be either inside or outside of the attack and can leave your opponent more vulnerable to your counterattack. Once you have practiced attacking with the angle punches in the following sequences, you can then do the same thing by having a partner attack you straight on while you angle and intercept.

You should also practice punching at different angles with or without the focus glove. To understand angles better, have the trainer stand there and let you hit at him without contact. This will illuminate the angle relationship between you and a possible opponent. It's also useful to do this with focus gloves.

Step Left and Punch

A: Dennis Blue is in a left lead facing the student, Jeremy Lynch.

B: Lynch steps out to the left and strikes Blue between the arms.

Right Curved Punch

A: Lynch and Blue face off.

B: Lynch curves right as he punches. Learn a similar technique on pages 42-43 of Volume 1.

Reacting to Distance

The purpose of this drill is to react to a target at different distances and with the proper penetration and little preparation. In reality, this drill can be done with any hand or kicking tool. The drill can be done stationary or while moving.

In this drill, the trainer has two focus gloves. He flashes one or both of them at different distances, and the student hits the gloves at the proper distance. The trainer initially holds the gloves at his chest so the student can't know what distance he plans to move them to. The drill can be done stationary. For example, the trainer could move the glove to a distance where it makes more sense for the student to execute a backfist or hook. Or the drill can be done while moving; the trainer does footwork to force the student to keep the fighting measure. When the student hits the glove, the trainer moves back or parries to force a counterattack. Or the trainer could move forward, forcing the student to hit while backing up. And there are many other possibilities.

In a variation, do the drill with the eyes closed. The trainer moves around while the student has his eyes closed and is waiting in the fighting stance. The trainer will then stop moving and yell, "Go!" The student opens his eyes and hits the focus glove. He may have to adapt his distance with a step-back punch, right curved punch, etc.

Flash-Glove Drill (Stationary)

A: Dennis Blue (right) is the trainer. He will remain stationary and flash the focus gloves at different distances.

B: Blue flashes a focus glove at a distance that Jeremy Lynch can still hit while stationary.

C: In this example, both the student and the trainer have recovered to their original positions. Blue could also have moved back or to the side and flashed a different distance for Lynch to strike.

D: Blue flashes his focus glove again, but this time he extends his shoulder so the glove reaches farther. Lynch must adjust by taking a slight step back with his rear foot to hit with the correct distance.

Flash-Glove Drill (Moving)

  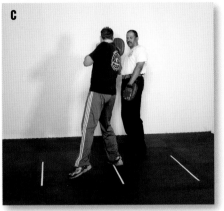

A: Acting as the trainer, Blue holds the focus glove as Lynch faces him at the fighting measure.

B: Blue moves to the right.

C: As soon as Lynch sees Blue move, he follows with a punch to the focus glove. This drill is difficult to do; you have to react to the movement and judge the distance for the hit at the same time. Try to go for a snappy 2-inch penetration with your hit.

Hitting-When-the-Trainer-Stops Drill

A: Blue and Lynch do the mirror drill. (See page 25.)

B: Lynch pivots to the right, following Blue.

C: When Blue stops moving, Lynch strikes.

Intercepting High and Low Attacks

Wednesday Night Group instructor Jim McCann came up with this drill to help students work on intercepting an opponent's high or low attack. This drill has proven very useful because it gives students the opportunity to practice against standing attacks as well as attacks where a grappler may shoot in for a takedown.

The drill begins with the trainer and student at the fighting measure. The trainer is in a left lead because many trained fighters—mixed martial artists, *muay Thai* fighters, boxers—fight in a left lead. In this example, the focus glove is in the right rear hand. By having the focus glove on the rear hand, it is even with the trainer's head. This makes the drill more realistic because the student intercepts at the same distance he would if he were really trying to hit an opponent's head. You can also practice this drill by having the trainer in a right lead with the focus glove in the left hand. The trainer steps forward with his lead leg. He could also step forward with his rear leg while holding the focus glove high and steady to mimic a straight lead punch and bridge the gap. The student intercepts the attack.

Once you can do the basics easily, the trainer will then execute either a high or low attack. The trainer should start the drill by attacking slowly and then build up to full speed, depending on when he feels the student is ready for it. Later, the trainer can fake or feint to train the student to not respond to false attacks.

Intercepting a High-Line Attack

A: Dennis Blue and Tim Tackett Jr. face each other in fighting stances.

B: When Blue steps forward with his left foot, he simulates a high attack. Tackett Jr. intercepts it with a straight lead punch.

Intercepting a Low-Line Attack

A: Blue and Tackett Jr. face each other in fighting stances.

B: This time Blue simulates a low attack, and Tackett Jr. intercepts it with a straight lead.

Using Footwork

A: Blue and Tackett Jr. face each other in fighting stances. Blue is the trainer.

B: This time Tackett Jr. uses footwork to avoid the attack by stepping laterally.

C: Tackett Jr.'s left leg immediately follows his right leg to recover his fighting stance. Note: You don't usually want to cross one leg in front of the other because you run the risk of being hit while you are in a weak position with no base. If you end up doing it, execute it as quickly as possible.

Speed and Snap

In combat, you can try to hit through a target or snap the punch with a few inches of penetration; both methods work. When you see a boxing match and someone is hit and knocked backwards, he has been hit with a punch that goes through the target. If you see him get hit and drop straight down, he has been hit with a snappy punch. At close range, JKD practitioners usually want to hit through the target because it is difficult to get full snap of the elbow. They will hit through the target by focusing on their punch going out the back of the opponent's head. (See the Palm Hook, Hammer Fist section on page 64).

This is a basic JKD drill used to work on the speed and snap of a punch from any range by hitting a piece of suspended paper. Bruce Lee believed this was a good drill because the paper gives no resistance. This means the student cannot push the paper; to hit it correctly, he has to snap.

To do this drill, you can have a partner hold the paper or just hang it up. Have it hang at head height.

Grabbing the paper serves the same purpose as hitting it. The only difference is that grabbing forces you to snap the punch back. This drill also allows you to work on getting rid of your preparation, as the trainer can pull his hand with the paper away if you telegraph the grab. Once the student can grab the paper with ease, the trainer can start to move his hand to make it harder for him to succeed. This will help teach the student to have little or no preparation when he hits.

It's also possible to do this drill with a candle, which is an old kung fu exercise. Snap a punch just a few inches above the flame to try to put out the candle. The breeze from the snap should extinguish it. Make sure you don't make any contact with the flame and burn yourself or something else.

Hitting-Paper Drill

A: Dennis Blue (left) holds a piece of paper at the height of Tim Tackett Jr.'s head.

B: Tackett Jr. push-steps and hits the paper with a straight lead punch.

C: He then recovers his fighting stance.

Grab-the-Paper Drill

A: Jeremy Lynch (right) holds a folded piece of paper in his right hand. Tim Tackett stands far enough away so that he can grab it with a fully extended straight lead hand without needing to take a step forward.

B: Tackett grabs the paper.

C: He recovers his position. Tackett and Lynch could also do the drill wherein Tackett needs to take a lead step or push forward.

Attacking on Preparation

This drill consists of the trainer and the student facing each other with focus gloves on their rear hands. The trainer starts a straight lead punch. The student responds simultaneously with the same punch. This reaction drill works on the speed of the student's ability to intercept an attack. The student should be able to learn to react so fast that an observer would not be able to tell which practitioner punched first.

Simultaneous Punch Drill

A: Tim Tackett Jr. and Dennis Blue face each other in fighting stances.

B: They appear to execute a punch at the same time, so it is unclear who is the student and who is the trainer.

Moving Off the Centerline

Anytime you attack, you run into the danger of a counterattack, and this is why you want to practice moving off the centerline. It makes it harder for the opponent to hit you with a counterattack because it's harder for him to know where your head will be.

Learn to do this with a trainer. The trainer will force the student to move by hitting at him with a focus glove, but only after the student has punched the glove with a straight lead or rear punch. In counterattacking, the student will have to learn to avoid it or defend himself. As mentioned in the Training Tips section of this chapter, you should work slowly at first.

Inside Slip Against the Counterattack

A: Tim Tackett Jr. and Dennis Blue square off in fighting stances.

B: Tackett Jr. executes a straight lead punch to Blue's rear glove.

C: Blue attacks on recovery with a straight lead punch.

D: Tackett Jr. slips inside the punch and counterstrikes with a straight rear punch. Because this is practice, he uses enough control to not make contact with his partner.

The Straight Rear Punch

Once you've worked on the straight lead punch, you can move on to the straight rear punch. The straight rear punch uses the same principles as the straight lead, except it is done with the rear arm and is generally considered a natural follow-up attack to the straight lead. Learn more about the straight rear punch on pages 43-44 of Volume 1.

You definitely want hip power when executing a straight rear punch. This drill helps students learn to use hip power by having them start with their lead arm fully extended, as if they have just executed a straight lead punch. You should practice this drill from as many different distances and combinations as are functional. For example, follow up with the straight rear after an opponent has blocked or parried your initial hit.

From there, you can expand the drill by doing the straight rear punch in combinations. The 1 – 2 combination (a straight lead punch followed by a straight rear) is a basic boxing combination. However, a boxer would use a minor blow (like the jab) to set up a more powerful blow (like a hook). In jeet kune do, practitioners try to go from major blow to major blow. Sometimes you will see JKD practitioners doing a sort of jab and straight rear punch combination. You'll hear the focus glove make a sound like "pop-POP" when they hit it. Instead, you want the sounds to go, "POP-POP," or even better, "POP-pop." Don't hurry through the first punch. Do it with power.

A variation of the straight rear punch is the overhead rear punch. It's valuable because it can go over an opponent's guard. It's also useful to slip inside an opponent's punch. Think of it as an exaggerated cross, except that it is more of a downward punch.

Straight Rear Punch

A: Tim Tackett Jr. has his lead arm extended as if he's just executed a straight lead punch.

B: He swings the left side of his body, as if he were a door that just slammed, to get the maximum power with his straight rear punch.

1 – 2 Combination

A: Dennis Blue holds the focus gloves for Tim Tackett Jr.

B: Tackett Jr. throws a right straight lead punch.

C: He follows it up with a straight rear punch. Note: Both punches should penetrate the focus glove approximately two inches to get the maximum snap in the punches.

Overhead Rear Punch

A: Tackett Jr. gets closer to Blue, his trainer.

B: Tackett Jr. throws an overhead rear punch.

C: He makes contact with the focus glove.

The Hook

Hooks are essential Western boxing elements in jeet kune do. Like other Western boxing punches, hooks are basic close-range punches that allow you to attack from different angles. They add variety to your attacks and are an important part of combinations. There is no hard and fast rule as to when you use them or start integrating them into your practice. Generally, the Wednesday Night Group waits until students have achieved some skill with the straight lead before adding other boxing elements.

To execute a hook, you need to rotate your body, as if you were in a barrel, while transferring weight to your rear leg. It's the quick twist of your body and weight going to the rear leg that gives the punch its power. The first picture sequence will demonstrate a few ways to practice that in training. The rest will demonstrate how to improve and develop its power. Learn more about the hook on page 50 of Volume 1.

Basic Hook

A: The basic hook is a close-range attack and is best used after bridging the gap with a longer-range strike like the straight lead punch or after moving inside the attack of an opponent. Here, Dennis Blue faces the trainer Tim Tackett Jr. close enough to the target that he does not have to step forward.

B: Blue makes contact with the focus glove with a hook punch by quickly rotating his body and by putting his weight on his rear leg.

Inside Slip Against a Straight Rear Punch

A: This is a defense drill. Tackett Jr. holds the focus gloves for Blue.

B: Tackett Jr. attempts to hit Blue with a straight rear punch with his rear focus glove.

C: Blue slips left and counterattacks with a hook.

Fade Back Against a Straight Lead Punch

A: This is another defense drill. Tackett Jr. faces Blue, the student.

B: Tackett Jr. attacks with a lead punch, but Blue fades back by putting his weight on his rear leg.

C: While fading back, Blue hits the focus glove with a front hook.

Bob and Weave

A: Blue bobs and weaves under Tackett Jr.'s hook.

B: To bob and weave, Blue slips inside Tackett Jr.'s hook.

C : He then counters with a hook of his own.

Elbow-on-Palm Power Drill

A

B

A: In order to learn how to get power from a short distance with the hook, Blue places his elbow on Tackett Jr.'s palm. Blue's fist is on the same level as the focus glove.

B: Blue then punches the glove with a hook and all the power he can muster; the drill forces him to use his hip to rotate into the punch. Note: The drill also shows how you can still get power from a short distance without winding up your striking arm.

Arm-on-Arm Power Drill

A

B

A: This drill is similar to the elbow-on-palm drill, but this time Blue's lead arm is inside Tackett Jr.'s before hitting.

B: Blue then hits the focus glove by shifting his weight to his back foot. This is another way to work on short-range power.

Extended-Straight-Rear-to-Hook Power Drill

A: Blue holds his rear arm fully extended at Tackett Jr.'s chest, as if he has just completed a straight rear punch.

B: He then pivots to hit the focus glove with a hook. In doing so, Blue obtains the maximum twist and follow-through for his hook because the drill works on rotating the body with full speed and power.

Close-Range Hook Power Drill

A: Tackett Jr. holds the focus glove at Blue's head. He does this so Blue will have to adjust his distance to execute a hook by fading back and putting his weight on his rear leg as he makes contact.

B: Blue drops his weight onto his rear leg to hit the focus glove with a hook.

Jut-and-Hit Power Drill

A: Jeremy Lynch is the student. Dennis Blue is the trainer. Lynch's hands are outside Blue's for a *jut sao* (jerking-hand technique) exercise.

B: When Blue moves to raise his arms, Lynch jerks them down.

C: Lynch follows up with a delayed hook. Learn more about the jut sao on pages 137-140 of Volume 1.

Palm Hook, Hammer Fist

The bones in your hands are delicate, and in a fight, you're constantly in danger of breaking them. The palm hook and hammer fist are two punches that help alleviate that danger.

The palm hook is thrown the same way as the boxing-type hook. The only difference is that you will hit your target with your palm instead of your fist. The advantage of the palm hook is that there is much less chance of injuring your hand. When hitting with a hook to the head, it is very easy to miss the jaw, hit the skull and hurt your hand. The bones of the fist are more fragile than the palm and can break when contacting a hard object like the head. Even boxers with boxing gloves have been known to break their hands when hitting a hard skull. (Hitting with the palm is called "palming" in boxing and is illegal.)

When hitting with a palm hook, make sure you make contact with the meat of your palm and not your fingers; the meat of your palm can withstand more force. The palm hook is not a snappy technique, but a heavy one. This means the hit will penetrate more than a snappy hit, but it will not snap back. Bruce Lee tended to call snappy hits "crispy" and heavy hits "uncrispy." While a crispy hit depends on speed and snap for power, an uncrispy hit depends on the weight going into the target. Palm-hook with as much dead weight as possible so that power goes into the target. Because the palm hook will penetrate, you don't need to consciously achieve the regular 2-inch penetration.

Practice the palm hook and other heavy hits by keeping your arm relaxed—think of your arm as very heavy—and then hitting through the target. Remember, you'll need more time to recover, so you'll be vulnerable to a counterattack. This is also why it's difficult to do the palm hook in combination with other punches. Generally, you only want to use it when you know you can make contact.

The other difference from the boxing hook is that you don't rotate your body and put your weight onto your rear leg. Instead, keep the weight on your front foot by digging your toes into the ground. This will help you drop weight into the punch.

The hammer fist is similar to the backfist. The main difference is that you make contact with the side of your fist instead of the backside or knuckles. The hammer fist is also safer to execute than the backfist because unless a backfist is accurate, you stand a good chance of breaking your hand.

Palm Hook

A: Dennis Blue faces his trainer, Jeremy Lynch.

B: Blue drops weight into his lead foot and executes a palm hook.

Hammerfist

A: Dennis Blue faces his trainer, Jeremy Lynch.

B: Blue executes a hammer fist. Notice the angle of his strike.

The Uppercut and the Shovel Hook

Like hooks, the uppercut and the shovel hook are close-range punches from Western boxing. These two punches are very similar in the way they are performed. The main difference is that the angle of the uppercut is horizontal, while the shovel hook is on a diagonal line. They are important in combinations and adding variety to your attack. There is no rule as to when you should integrate them into your training, but the Wednesday Night Group generally recommends you achieve some proficiency in your straight lead punch first. Both are good follow-up techniques and are used in attack combinations. They are also some of the main punches that are used after getting inside an opponent's own attack or fighting measure. The exercises and drills in this section are designed to help you get power in these punches and to help you practice using these tools in combat. Any of the drills below can be done with either the shovel hook or uppercut. Learn more about the uppercut on page 51 of Volume 1. Learn more about the shovel hook on page 52 of Volume 1.

The Uppercut

A: Dennis Blue is close enough to the target to execute an uppercut.

B: Blue lowers his body by putting his weight mostly on his right leg.

C: Driving off his right leg, he hits the focus glove with an uppercut.

Elbow-on-Palm Drill

A: Jeremy Lynch rests his elbow on the palm of Dennis Blue's lead hand.

B: Lynch hits the focus glove with a shovel hook by driving upward with his front leg for power. In doing so, Lynch is learning how to explode from a relaxed position.

Counter Punch With Shovel Hook

A: To practice the shovel hook, Blue (the trainer) faces Lynch.

B: Blue tries to hit Lynch with a straight lead punch.

C: Lynch slips to the outside of the punch, then attacks Blue's exposed side with a shovel hook.

Combination-Punching Drills

Once you are able to do the above punches with some efficiency, you should start putting them together in combinations. Attacking by combination, which mixes hand and kicking tools, is one of the Five Ways of Attack taught by Bruce Lee. The purpose of this section of the book is to give you an idea of various ABC hand attacks. Learn more about attacks by combination on pages 109-114 of Volume 1.

In combination-punching drills, the trainer will hold two focus gloves. He will feed the student combination punches by the way he holds the focus gloves. Some basic combinations include:

- straight lead to straight rear
- straight lead to front hook
- straight lead to rear uppercut or shovel hook
- front uppercut to front hook
- front uppercut to rear uppercut
- front hook to straight rear
- straight lead to rear overhead
- straight lead to front uppercut
- front high hook to front low hook

When feeding the focus gloves to the student, the trainer can remain stationary, move forward so the student can practice moving backward, move backward so the student can learn to keep forward pressure, mix footwork, and/or circle. The trainer can also attack with one focus glove so the student can practice hit-and-parry or parry-and-hit combinations. When training in such a manner, the student should try to avoid blocking without hitting because it gives the opponent time to renew his attack. Remember—whenever possible, intercept.

Once you can execute two-punch combinations with speed, power and balance with little to no preparation, you can progress to three-punch combinations. A common three-punch combination is jab-cross-hook from Western boxing or straight lead-straight rear-front hook in jeet kune do.

Also remember, that combinations are a great way to practice defense against punches. The trainer throws a combination while the student defends against it. The sequences below illustrate two examples.

Intercepting a Right Lead Front Hook

A: Jeremy Lynch holds focus gloves for Tim Tackett Jr.

B: Lynch throws a high hook that Tackett Jr. tries to parry.

C: If Tackett Jr. is slow to react, he can parry and hit at the same time to intercept the attack.

Intercepting an Unmatched Left Lead Hook

A: Lynch faces Tackett Jr. in a left lead.

B: When Lynch throws a left hook, Tackett Jr. intercepts it with a sliding-leverage vertical-hook attack. Learn more about sliding leverage on pages 84-86 of Volume 1.

Straight-Blast Drills

A basic follow-up to an interception is the straight blast. Generally, if you've dazed your opponent with an attack or counterattack, you'll probably use a flurry of straight blasts to end the encounter.

There are several ways to do a blast—with your shoulders squared like in *wing chun*, or with a twist of your shoulders and hips in jeet kune do. Your choice will depend on the distance between you and your opponent. Wing chun blasts are shorter and snappier and have a faster recovery. JKD blasts are made for distance and power. Experiment with both to find which works best for you and under what circumstances. Learn more about straight blasts on pages 45-49 of Volume 1.

To train for distance, power and follow-up, use focus gloves with a trainer who is stationary, mixes footwork, uses different angles and fights back. You can improve the snap of a blast with your back to the mat. Keep your shoulder on the floor while you punch the focus gloves. It will force you to snap your punch from your elbow.

At the Wednesday Night Group, we like to train blasts in rounds of 1 minute or longer. By working in timed rounds, you work on physical conditioning as well as perfecting the blast itself. When working with the blasts, as with any tool, try to see if you can do two or more things at once. You'll quickly discover that a few rounds of straight-blast practice are difficult enough, but you can make it harder by throwing in a specific exercise. For example, do 20 push-ups and then 40 straight blasts on the focus gloves. Repeat two or three times.

Wing Chun Blast to JKD Blast

A: Tim Tackett is too close to his trainer to do a JKD blast.

B: Instead, he does a *wing chun* blast to gain distance.

C: The wing chun blasts pushes the trainer back.

D, E: Now Tackett has enough distance to do JKD blasts.

Shove to JKD Blast

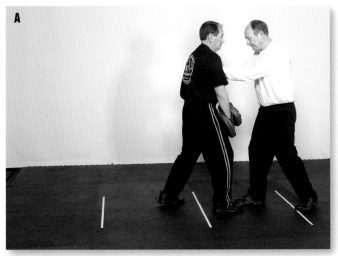

A: Tackett is the student in this drill. He is too close to his trainer to launch an attack, so he shoves him to get the proper distance.

B: As soon as he is shoved back, the trainer raises the focus gloves.

C, D, E: Now that he has the proper distance, Tackett hits with a series of JKD blasts.

Blast to Boxing Combinations

A: After doing two or more blasts, the trainer adds to Tackett's practice by feeding him boxing combinations, beginning with a hook.

B: The trainer feeds Tackett a straight rear punch.

C: Then he feeds him an uppercut. Note: Sometimes an opponent will cover up when being attacked by blasts. That's when this drill will come in handy; you'll know how to use boxing combinations to break up his defense.

JKD Blasts to Knee Attacks

A: Jeremy Lynch faces his trainer, Dennis Blue.

B, C, D: Lynch executes three JKD blasts.

E: Then Blue lowers the focus gloves, giving Lynch the signal to transition to knee strikes.

F: Lynch puts his right hand on Blue's shoulder as he makes contact with his right knee. He does this to measure the distance and to keep his opponent from moving forward.

Blasts on the Kicking Shield

A: To add to variety in training, Lynch and Blue blast on the kicking shield.

B: Lynch hits with a series of blasts while Blue holds the shield.

C: Note: If they were in class with multiple trainer-student pairs, Lynch and Blue could practice on the kicking shield while the other group uses the focus gloves. After a certain time or number of rounds, they could switch.

Getting Distance, No. 1

A, B: Sometimes opponents cover up and are hard to hit. To open his opponent's defense, Lynch shoves his trainer Blue back.

C, D: He could also use blasts to create distance.

E: This could also give Lynch the distance necessary to kick his trainer.

Getting Distance, No. 2

A, B: Starting with the focus gloves close, Lynch needs to create distance with blasts.

C, D: He moves from wing chun blasts to JKD blasts.

Aggressive Jimmy-Jam Drills

Since you can't always be at the perfect distance, jimmy-jam drills from basic boxing training will help. They are valuable because they force the student to react to the trainer hitting at him with the glove. They also force the student to lower his body and hit with power. Lowering the body is one way boxers work on punching with power. In jeet kune do, practitioners lower their bodies at close range to add weight to their punches. The harder the trainer hits with the glove, the heavier the punch has to be to counter the force coming at him. When hitting the glove, the student should make sure to meet it no more than halfway between his head or body. The trainer may also choose to go with the glove only halfway to the target, stop, or attempt to follow through if the student isn't fast enough to intercept the strike.

When doing this drill, use the softer type of focus glove to avoid injuring your hand. It may also be a good idea to wrap your hands or wear MMA gloves, especially if your hands are not used to hitting with heavy contact. You need to feel that you are punching as hard as possible and know that you will not suffer any damage. You don't want to subconsciously hold back on the power of the hit.

In boxing, the various punches are given a number. This allows the trainer to call out those punches and combinations more easily.

In the Wednesday Night Group, we use the following numbers: (1) straight lead punch or jab, (2) straight rear punch or cross, and (3) hook. Once the student can do all three numbers separately and from a stationary position, the trainer then feeds them in a random order. Once the student can do the drill while stationary, the trainer then moves in all directions. The trainer can also call out the various numbers and combinations.

Jimmy-Jam Drill

A, B: Dennis Blue feeds the front focus glove for a No. 1. Jeremy Lynch intercepts it with a straight lead punch.

C, D: Blue feeds the rear glove, which is the signal for a straight rear punch (No. 2). Lynch intercepts it with a No. 2.

E, F: Blue feeds Lynch a hook (No. 3), and Lynch responds with a hook. Dennis then feeds the hook line (No. 3), and Jeremy responds with a hook.

This chapter has a lot of drills, and many of them can be redesigned to include or apply to other JKD tools. In fact, it's a good idea to take straight-lead-punch drills and see if they're useful for other tools. Don't be afraid to adapt them. For example, you may find that the 1-to-5 drill is good for working on your side kick. Also, once you've worked on some drills, make sure to try them with footwork or with a fake/feint before or after kicks.

You may find only some of the drills useful to your individual skills, or if you're an instructor, to those of your class. Because each student is different, trainers who teach classes may find it difficult to stop an entire class to help one student who is having trouble. In that case, trainers may want to help the student separately and have them practice outside of class. Or they can do what Bruce Lee did: give each student a report on their progress with specific drills and exercises to improve their areas of weakness. First-generation JKD student Bob Bremer, who is coauthor of *Chinatown Jeet Kune Do Volume 1*, still has the ones Bruce Lee wrote for him.

Chapter 4
KICKING TOOLS

In the Wednesday Night Group, we start out new students with basic fighting stances and footwork. From there, we add basic hand attacks, like the straight lead and rear punch. At the same time the student begins to learn basic hand tools, they also begin to learn about basic kicks. Basic tools are the techniques that seemed to be used most often in sparring and self-defense practice. They are the primary tools of your JKD training. The primary kicks are:

- the scoop kick
- the front thrust kick
- the hook kick
- the inverted hook kick
- the side kick

Of course, you may find that other kicks work better as primary ones for you. The above list is what the Wednesday Night Group trains first. Students learn to use each primary kick against a high and low target.

To avoid injury when practicing kicks, make sure you warm up and stretch out before doing any kicking exercises. This is particularly important when you work on high kicks. Of course, JKD practitioners generally don't kick above the waist, but they do practice higher kicks for the following reasons:

- If you can hook-kick both high and low quickly and accurately, then you can work on defending against both high and low attacks.
- It's difficult to learn to defend against high kicks if no one in the class can do them.
- It adds variety to your attacks.
- Working on high kicks can help your balance, flexibility and conditioning.

Many of the drills shown in the hand tools chapter can be done with the various kicking tools. For example, any of the distance drills can be done with kicks.

To learn more about the concepts behind specific kicking tools, feel free to cross-reference Chapter 4 in Volume 1. Otherwise, when training in the drills in this book, most of them start at the fighting measure, although you can try them at other distances. Any drill that starts at the fighting measure means that you'll probably want to recover after kicking. Make sure you vary your rhythm. The drills should start slow and pick up speed. As discussed in the last chapter, the person overseeing the drill will be identified as the trainer, while the person doing the drill will be identified as the student.

Training Tips

When working on your kicks, try to keep them light and easy without straining or using more muscle power than necessary. Make sure your kicks are quick and direct for efficiency. Use proper body torque to get powerful kicks, but at the same time, don't telegraph your intent by leaning back, moving your arms, etc. Practice good balance before, during and after your kick, and remember to cover yourself from execution to recovery. You want to develop your kicks so you can use them as a quick reaction as well as a counter.

Start your training by having the student kick a focus glove; in all the drills, you'll notice how the trainer holds the focus glove in the correct manner for each kick. From there, students can practice kicks from a stationary stance or from the fighting measure, wherein he must slide up to make contact. Because kicking is a much larger movement than a punch, the student will need to watch his telegraphed preparation. And while low kicks have less preparation, they still have some. (Note: That's why you'll often see JKD practitioners disguise preparation with a hand feint.) This is why the trainer needs to look out to help the student get rid of as much preparation as possible. He also should look for accuracy and power in the student's kicks. Of course, a proper snappy kick will make a loud pop on the focus glove.

Finally, experiment with switching lead legs when you kick. Or experiment by staying in the same lead. Take the scoop kick for example: You execute the kick with your lead leg, then recover to the opposite lead to execute another kick from that leg. Or you could slide up to scoop-kick with your lead leg, recover, then hook-kick with your rear left leg. Switching leads will add variety to your kicking attack and make it harder for your opponent to defend against them. You could also vary your kicking attacks by using pendulum footwork to return to the fighting measure. Or you can step straight down to punch. Learn more about the pendulum kick on page 63 of Volume 1.

Basic Kicks

Start training kicks with the focus glove in basic kicking drills. In these drills, the basic kicks start from a fighting stance. Make sure you keep your balance and recover back to a proper stance. Try to stay as relaxed as possible. Go slow at first and try to hit the focus glove with precision. When you feel you are doing the kick correctly, you can add more force and speed to the kick.

Basic kicking drills work on three main areas. The first is accuracy, because the focus glove is small and must be hit exactly. The second is power, because the student can work on hitting the focus glove as hard as possible without worrying about hurting the trainer. And the third is execution. Because the trainer will be able to watch the entire kick from start to finish, he'll point out any errors.

Scoop Kick (Same Lead)

A: Vince Raimondi (right) and Patrick Cunningham stand at the fighting measure. Patrick Cunningham holds the focus gloves for a scoop kick.

B: Raimondi slides up a little to make initial contact with his instep.

C: Raimondi then scoops up his toes, which makes a powerful snapping action.

D: Raimondi slides back to recover his original position with the same lead forward. Learn more about the scoop kick on pages 68-69 of Volume 1.

Scoop Kick (Switching Leads)

A: Raimondi and Cunningham stand at the fighting measure. Cunningham holds the focus gloves for a scoop kick.

B: Raimondi executes a basic scoop kick.

C: He recovers to the opposite lead leg stance.

Hook Kick (Telegraphic)

A: Raimondi is in a fighting stance. Cunningham holds the focus gloves for a hook kick.

B: Raimondi exaggerates chambering his kicking leg for the purpose of this exercise. The exaggeration helps him work on balance and forces him to use his hip when kicking.

C: Raimondi hook-kicks the target.

D: He chambers his kicking leg.

E: Raimondi recovers his fighting stance. Learn more about the hook kick on pages 70-72 of Volume 1.

Hook Kick (Nontelegraphic)

A: Eventually, the JKD practitioner will hook-kick from a natural bend. Jeremy Lynch (right) will demonstrate from the fighting stance.

B: A natural-bend hook kick is less telegraphic, which means Lynch's trainer won't be able to read the exact angle or kick he plans to use.

Inverted Hook Kick

A: Vince Raimondi is in a fighting stance, while the trainer, Patrick Cunningham, is holding a focus glove in the correct position.

B: As with the hook kick, Raimondi chambers his kicking leg. Note: Experiment with how much you want to chamber your kicking leg. There is no hard and fast rule for which is best. Try all angles and do what works for you.

C: Raimondi executes an inverted hook kick.

D: He snaps his foot back.

E: Raimondi returns to his fighting stance. Learn more about the inverted hook kick on page 71 of Volume 1.

Side Kick

A: Raimondi is in a fighting stance facing his trainer, Cunningham, who is holding the focus gloves at the proper angle.

B: Raimondi slides up and prepares to side-kick.

C: At the same time, he twists his hips and slides his grounded foot to execute a side kick at the focus glove.

D: Raimondi snaps his kicking leg back.

E: This time Raimondi brings his leg straight down so he can deliver a hand attack. Note: It may look like Raimondi's telegraphing his side kick, but remember that the execution should really occur in a split second. Learn more about the side kick on pages 58-64 of Volume 1.

Inward Crescent Kick

A: From the fighting measure, Raimondi (left) prepares to execute an inward crescent kick.

B: He slides up to bridge the gap.

C: Raimondi executes the inward crescent kick by swinging his lead leg in a counterclockwise arc.

D: After kicking the focus glove, Raimondi steps straight down.

E: He could also pendulum back to the fighting measure. Learn more about the inward crescent kick on page 72 of Volume 1.

Outward Crescent Kick

A: Raimondi prepares to do an outside crescent kick from the fighting measure. Cunningham holds the focus glove in the appropriate position.

B: After sliding up with his rear leg, Raimondi does the outside crescent kick by swinging his leg in a clockwise arc.

C: Raimondi steps straight down after the kick. He could also pendulum back to the fighting measure. Learn more about the outward crescent kick on page 73 of Volume 1.

Flip Kick

A: Dennis Blue will execute the close-range flip kick. Jeremy Lynch holds the focus gloves at the proper position. In a real fight, however, the flip kick comes at such an unusual angle that it's hard for an opponent to see.

B: Blue slides up to get in close.

C: Keeping his lead knee down, Blue flips the lower part of his leg up to hit the focus glove with the outer edge of his foot. In a real fight, his target would be the groin.

Reaction, Speed and Accuracy

Once you have the basic kicks down, you can focus on exercises that develop reaction, speed and accuracy by training with a moving focus glove. I'll use the hook kick as an example, but you can use any kick. Do the drill as follows:

From the fighting measure, the trainer has the focus glove in the correct hook-kick position. He takes a step forward to bridge the gap, and the student intercepts it with a hook kick. If the step forward takes one beat, the kick should be executed on the half-beat. In other words, if someone were to say "one" out loud as the trainer steps forward, the student should land his kick on the "wuh" sound.

Imagine doing the same action as before, but this time, the trainer steps back. The student will have to use footwork to close the distance and be in range to make contact.

Assume the same action again, but this time the trainer steps forward or back, and the student adjusts to the distance and kicks. To make the drill more complex, he could step side-to-side, push-step or pivot. But start out simple!

Power Kicking (Half-Kick Drills)

The half-kick drills are an important part of the Wednesday Night Group kick training because they help students learn to kick with power. They were developed by JKD instructor Jeremy Lynch in an effort to get his students to kick harder; they force the students to use hip, shoulder and foot rotation. This drill only uses half of the basic hook-kick drill on page 83. That's why it's called a "half-kick" drill. It starts with the student standing on one leg with the knee bent at the same angle the student would use if he were about to kick. He is facing the trainer and can reach the glove with the kick without having to move forward. This makes the drill difficult to do because at first it is hard to keep your balance and get any power at all. Try to keep working on it until you can hear a loud pop on the focus glove. We use the hard-surface type of glove for this drill. You can experiment with many different kinds of kicks.

For whipping kicks, like the hook kick, you want the knee to go past the target before you make contact with the focus glove. For other kicks, like the side kick, you will use the water-hose principle, in which you penetrate the target only four to six inches. Note: If you want your opponent to be kicked back farther with the water-hose principle, you can penetrate farther.

Half Hook Kick

A: Dennis Blue holds the focus glove for Jeremy Lynch.

B: Lynch gets into position by standing with his weight on his rear leg. He is close enough to the target to make contact with a kick without having to move forward.

C: To execute his kick, Lynch must raise his right leg while balancing on his left. He must twist his rear foot and torque his body by throwing his right hip and shoulder in the direction of the focus glove. He wants to penetrate four to six inches beyond the focus glove with a fast, snappy kick.

D: Lynch snaps his foot back to where he started.

Half Inverted Hook Kick

A: Blue holds the focus glove in the correct position.

B: Lynch sets up his kick by balancing on his rear foot.

C: Lynch snaps his leg and hip to the right. Because this is a hook kick, he wants his knee to move past the target before he makes contact.

D: Lynch returns to his original position and is ready to kick again.

Half Scoop Kick

A: Lynch balances on his rear leg, preparing for a scoop kick. Blue holds the focus glove at the proper angle.

B: Lynch kicks with a lot of snap, as if his leg were a whip.

C: Lynch returns to his original position.

Kicking With Commitment

The more commitment you have in a kick or punch, the more power you have in your strike. However, that also means it will take you slightly longer to recover the fighting measure or to counterattack. In the Wednesday Night Group, we stress that students only attempt a full-commitment attack if they can land it with accuracy and power. Because it is harder to recover from a more committed kick, you must be sure you can use it with out being countered. Generally, that's only certain when your opponent is stunned or off-balance. In the Wednesday Night Group, students practice commitment with the hook kick but experiment on different levels of commitment with different kicks. Remember: More torque means more commitment and power!

Full-Commitment Hook Kick

A: In doing the full-commitment kick, Jeremy Lynch's rear foot is so twisted that it's facing the opposite direction of the kick. This twist follows the same idea as a baseball hitter swinging a bat, but in this case, the leg is the bat.

Half-Commitment Hook Kick

A: While the quick hook kick does not have as much power as the full-commitment one, it is a kick that is easier to recover from. From the fighting measure, Lynch quickly slides up and kicks with a snap of the knee. The difference with the more committed kick is that there is not as much rotation on the rear foot, so the recovery is faster.

Basic Stop-Kick Drill

A: Jeremy Lynch faces his trainer, Dennis Blue, who is holding a kicking shield. Lynch is in the natural stance.

B: When Blue steps forward, Lynch intercepts with a stop-kick.

C: He does a front thrust kick at full commitment. Learn more about the front thrust kick on page 69 of Volume 1.

The Side Kick

The kicking shield is one of the best ways to teach a student how to use the side kick. It's better than the focus glove because it is larger and not as frustrating for a beginner to learn to side kick on it. The shield also gives very good feedback to the trainer on the force of the kick, and it's a good way to kick something solid without injuring the trainer. When practicing the side kick on the kicking shield, the student is working on speed, accuracy, power, snap, proper penetration, lack of preparation and recovery. He is basically working on the complete development of the kick.

When working on the side kick, the student should start at a long distance from the trainer so he has to use a lead step and slide to hit the shield. The kick should penetrate between four and six inches. Any deeper than that and the student won't achieve any snap in the kick, which comes from the knee. Learn more about the side kick on pages 57-64 of Volume 1.

The student should practice getting closer and closer to the shield until he can place his hand on the shield and still have power—the hand lets the student know his close range. Getting enough snap in the kick requires as much momentum as possible. As an aid to this, snap down with your rear heel to help propel the kick.

Another good side kick drill is between two shields, especially for conditioning against more than one opponent. In this drill, the student stands between two shields and kicks them one after another until a specific number of kicks or a specific time limit has been reached. You can also do this drill with other kicks on the focus gloves.

Note: You want to be explosive when you side-kick. To practice this, jump with tuck jumps as high as possible three times. To do a tuck jump, jump straight up in the air and bring your knees to your chest. This is not only a good conditioning drill, but also helps with the explosion of the kick.

Side-Kick Shield Drill

A: Jeremy Lynch faces his trainer, Dennis Blue.

B: Lynch feints a finger jab to hide his preparation. Note: If Blue were to notice Lynch take a lead step, he should point it out.

C: Lynch slides up and kicks a split second before his rear foot touches the ground. Note: Lynch's rear foot is pointing away for the kick for maximum torque and stability. To test this, hold your side kick up while your partner is holding it. Have him push you with your foot at a 90-degree angle, then with the foot facing straight back. See which one gives you the most stability.

D: Lynch recovers the fighting measure.

Close-Range Side-Kick Shield Drill

A: Lynch places his hand on the shield to measure the distance.

B: To kick as fast as possible and still get power, Lynch side-kicks with a more natural bend of the leg.

C: Lynch completes the kick.

D: He then recovers back to a farther distance.

Kicks and Combinations

There are other ways to use the shields in practice with kicking combinations. Here are a few of them:

- Do the side kick in combination with other kicks.
- Throw a finger jab as a feint followed by a side kick.
- Have the trainer make a verbal or nonverbal cue so the student knows when to kick.
- Designate whether the trainer will mix footwork by retreating, moving forward so the student can intercept the shield, or moving back if he sees preparation.
- Make your own.

Combination: Side Kick to Hook Kick

A: Lynch faces Blue from the fighting measure.

B: He slides up to execute a side kick. Lynch wants to make sure he penetrates four to six inches.

C: Lynch recovers to the fighting measure. Notice how Blue adjusts his position with the shield.

D, E: Lynch executes a hook kick.

F: He recovers to the fighting measure.

Combination: Side Kick to Rear-Leg Hook

A: Lynch faces Blue from the fighting measure.

B: He slides up and executes a side kick.

C: He recovers his position. Notice how Blue doesn't change the shield's position.

D: Lynch executes a rear-leg hook kick.

Back-and-Forth Mirror Drills:

This drill has many purposes. First, it helps you learn to use distance when defending against a kick. Second, it helps you learn how to quickly counterattack with a kick of your own. Third, it helps you recognize what kick you are being attacked with and then instantly respond with the same kick.

To practice this drill, the student slides up with a kick while the trainer retreats just out of range. The trainer then returns the same kick, and the student retreats. They go back and forth until a specific time limit has been reached. Then the other student acts as the trainer and starts the drill with a different kick. The purpose of the drill is to recognize the kick, as the student does not know what kick will be thrown at him; he has to both retreat and have the balance to quickly return the same kick. The JKD practitioners can use any of the following ideas for this drill: low kicks with the front or rear leg, any foot-to-hand-tool combinations, any hand-to-foot-tool combinations, and any feint-to-kicking combinations.

Back-and-Forth Mirror Drill

A: Jeremy Lynch faces Dennis Blue.

B: Blue kicks at Lynch's shin with a low side kick.

C: Lynch retreats and Blue recovers.

D: Lynch mimics the same kick.

Back-and-Forth Focus-Glove Practice

The following drills are good for both reaction and recovery. This drill is the same as the back-and-forth mirror drill, but this time the trainer and student can work on power and accuracy as well as conditioning. You can also do these as timed rounds.

To do the drill: Both trainer and student have focus gloves, which they hold for the same kick. The trainer will then kick the glove and quickly recover to his starting position while the other student quickly follows with the same kick. He should try to kick the glove as the first man is recovering. You should go back and forth until a set number of kicks or a set time limit is reached. You can do this drill with side kicks, front kicks, inverted hook kicks, etc.

Back-and-Forth Front Kicks

A: Vince Raimondi and Patrick Cunningham face each other. They each hold focus gloves in their lead hands.

B: Cunningham executes a front kick.

C: Raimondi executes a front kick as an attack on recovery.

D: Raimondi completes the kick. Cunningham will try to execute a similar front kick on Raimondi's recovery.

Back-and-Forth Hook Kick

A: Raimondi and Cunningham face each other. They each hold focus gloves in their lead hands. Notice how the focus glove is positioned for a hook kick.

B: Cunningham moves to execute a hook kick.

C: He follows through with a hook kick.

D: While he recovers, Raimondi moves in to execute a hook kick.

E: He follows through with a hook kick.

F: Raimondi recovers, and Cunningham will then kick, and so on.

Advanced Kicking Drill

One of the hardest drills to do is one where the student starts the kick and then the trainer shows him what kick to do by flashing the focus glove. After students have a basic understanding of how to do a particular kick, they can start working all their kicks with the same method. This drill begins with the student starting the kick before the trainer flashes the glove. As the student starts the kick, he has to instantly see and then react with the correct kick. The purpose of this drill is that you may start a kick in a combat situation and see that you have to change the kick as it progresses toward the target. For example, you may start a scoop kick and notice that the opponent's arm is going to block it. You then go to whatever line he is now leaving open. The Wednesday Night Group picked up on this idea when Bob Bremer would talk about how Bruce Lee would start a kick to one part of the body and then be able to switch to another line in a split second.

Proper Kicking Placement

A, B: Dennis Blue slides up and cocks his leg. From this position, Blue should be able to start a kick and adjust the line the kick travels to match any possible opening in his opponent's defense.

Scoop Kick

A: Dennis Blue (left) faces his trainer, Jeremy Lynch.

B: Blue moves to his line to kick. Notice how Lynch now flashes the gloves to a scoop-kick position.

C: Blue executes a scoop kick.

D: Blue recovers to the fighting measure.

Low Hook Kick

A: Blue faces his trainer, Lynch.

B: He moves to his line. Lynch still hasn't signaled. Timing is obviously very important. Note: The whole drill should happen with no pause between the beginning and end. It should all look like one continuous kick.

C: When Lynch signals a low hook kick, Blue executes one.

Inverted Hook Kick

A: Blue faces his trainer, Lynch.

B: He moves to his line. Lynch hasn't signaled yet.

C: Lynch flashes the cue for an inverted hook kick, and Blue executes it.

Chase Drills

Chase drills teach students to attack a retreating opponent. In this chase drill, the student kicks at the trainer with a side kick (or any kick). In this case, the trainer does not have any equipment. The trainer uses distance to defend while the student attempts to close the distance with one or two more kicks.

If you want to use equipment, you can use focus gloves. The trainer moves back while holding the focus gloves. The student follows with kicks, attempting to make contact with the focus gloves.

To add difficulty to the drill, the trainer can also move forward, forcing the student to move back and get distance to kick. The trainer can then move forward and back while the student follows the glove.

———— ⌁ ————

Once you have worked on your basic tools and feel that you have a decent grasp on how to perform them with speed, power and dexterity, you can move on to the drills in the latter half of this book. If you don't feel that you are doing the punch or kick correctly, go back and practice some more.

Chapter 5
DEFENSES

If you ask almost anyone the main reason they take a martial art, they will usually say it's for defending against a possible attacker. The other main reason is health, and while the drills in this book promote health through exercise, it is an added benefit. That said, this chapter deals with the basic methods of JKD defense training, which uses boxing gloves in a controlled environment. The glove drills shown in this chapter are also a precursor to the sparring drills shown in Chapter 7. If you are a student new to martial arts, you should work on the various drills in this chapter before going on to the sparring chapter. The drills need to feel safe and comfortable, and the trainer should be careful when feeding any technique that can make physical contact. He should start slowly and then build up to full speed once the student shows that he can handle it. The great thing about this kind of training is that it benefits both partners. While one partner practices defense, the other can practice offense.

This chapter also adds to the information in Chapter 5 of Volume 1. It would be a good idea to review that chapter to better understand the concepts discussed in this one.

Training Tips

To really make your techniques efficient, you must work against an opponent who is really trying to hit you. Since this type of training can result in injury, you must start slow and easy. You should also be sure that you trust your training partner and that you work on helping each other. To do this, you will need to set your ego aside and realize that no matter how good you are, everyone gets hit at some point when they spar.

To make a student feel comfortable with contact training, start them out learning safety boxing drills. This type of training includes blocking, learning to roll with a punch and other passive moves. While passive moves should be avoided in self-defense situations, they are sometimes unavoidable. They can actually come in handy in real life, such as in an "oh crap" moment when you are caught unaware and have little time to do anything else but block or roll a punch. Otherwise, the defining characteristic of passive moves is that they give an opponent time to launch a second attack; if you block and hit, your opponent has the space needed to attack. That's why the basic method of JKD defense is to intercept an opponent's attack with a stop-hit or stop-kick.

From there, drill with straight lead punches, followed by straight rear punches, and then add hooks and other boxing punches. Always begin these drills from the fighting measure to give the student enough time to react. Then move closer until the trainer doesn't have to step forward. Defense is usually needed when your opponent has bridged the gap, and that's why you eventually want to practice your defense drills with the trainer executing techniques from close range.

While the matching-hands drills are all shown right lead against right lead, some time should be spent on left leads against left leads. The same is true when working on unmatched or left-to-right leads.

In regards to kicking, once the student has learned basic kicks with some speed and accuracy, you can start drilling defense. Like with hand tools, the trainer will hit with a punch or kick, and the student will react with the proper defense. After the student learns the basic defense from a stationary position, the trainer will use footwork to move and attack. Remember that you are only limited by your own imagination!

The Catch

Sometimes you may be unable to intercept a straight punch on time and are unable to use distance or angling to move off the line of attack. If this happens, you will be glad you spent a lot of time drilling the catch. Note: The catch is also more effective than a parry in a "too late" situation because it doesn't open up the centerline; it covers it.

To catch, the student puts the palm of a boxing glove in front of his chin facing outward. The trainer shoots a straight lead punch directly at the student's chin. The student catches the punch as if he were catching a fastball; he is not too stiff or too relaxed. He should not reach out for it with his glove but rather catch it with a slight pop forward. The trainer needs to make sure not to punch too fast or too hard. He can later pick up speed as the student improves. Once the student has worked against front-hand attacks like the straight lead, the trainer can start throwing straight rear punches.

Because the most common boxing attack is the lead jab, work on defending against it and the straight lead first. Then practice against the straight rear punch, which is harder to defend against in a boxing format, because your weak hand is forward. In any format, the straight rear punch will also be more telegraphic. Learn more about the catch on pages 86-88 of Volume 1.

Single-Catch Drill

A: Tim Tackett and Patrick Cunningham square off. Tackett has the boxing glove at his chin.

B: Cunningham steps forward and shoots a straight lead punch or jab. Tackett catches it with the palm of his glove.

Simultaneous-Hit Drill

A: Cunningham is bridging the gap with straight lead punches. This time Tackett will respond with a punch of his own.

B: As soon as Tackett senses a punch, he fires one of his own. Cunningham and Tackett catch each other's punches with their boxing gloves directly in front of their chins. Note: The simultaneous-hit drill teaches the student to react with a hit of his own. The trainer can start with some preparation to give the student a visual cue when to punch. Once the student can react quickly, the trainer can use less preparation so an observer wouldn't be able to tell who hit first.

The Double/Triple-Catch Drill

A: Tackett and Cunningham square off. Tackett has the boxing glove under his chin.

B: Cunningham shoots a straight lead punch, which Tackett catches.

C: Because this is a double-catch drill, Cunningham shoots another straight lead punch immediately after the first is caught.

D: For a triple-catch drill, Cunningham would shoot off a third punch.

Catch-and-Return Counterpunching Drill

A: Tackett and Cunningham will catch and trade punches. They will practice it in a rhythm. They also will move.

B: Cunningham throws a punch, and Tackett catches it.

C: Now Tackett counters with a punch, which Cunningham catches.

D: Cunningham returns the punch.

Catch Against a Straight Rear

A: Tackett and Cunningham face each other in fighting stances.

B, C: Cunningham executes a straight rear punch, which Tackett catches with his rear boxing glove.

Rolling Your Shoulder

Sometimes you are too close to your opponent to avoid being hit. You also may be too late to avoid, catch or intercept a hit. As with the catch, you can avoid being hit by rolling back and away from the punch. In boxing terminology, this is called a "shoulder roll." The shoulder roll is the main way to do this, especially to avoid the straight rear punch. You execute a shoulder roll by putting weight on your back leg and deflecting the punch with your forearm or shoulder. By moving the weight to your back leg, you move away from the punch. Sometimes, if you need to, you can even take a short step back with your rear leg as you do the shoulder roll.

As in other basic defense drills, the trainer will do a specific punch to a specific area while the student responds with the required technique. You can start by doing the drills from a stationary position and add footwork and movement later. Start with straight lead punches, then move on to hooks and other boxing techniques.

Shoulder Roll

A: Tim Tackett is a little too close to Patrick Cunningham to use distance or a counterattack.

B: Cunningham attempts to hit Tackett with a straight rear punch.

C: Tackett rolls his shoulder, causing him to fade back. He then parries the punch with his shoulder and upper arm, which helps to deflect the punch.

Shoulder Roll With Punch

A: Any shoulder roll can also lead to a counterattack because you are able to hit while retreating.

B: When Cunningham punches, Tackett fades back with a shoulder roll and hits with a straight lead punch over the top of Cunningham's strike.

Shoulder Roll With Side Kick

A: The shoulder roll sometimes provides the distance necessary to counterattack with a long-range kick. Here, Tackett attacks by drawing Cunningham's rear punch with his lead hand. Learn more about attack by drawing on pages 120-124 of Volume 1.

B: When Cunningham attempts his strike, Tackett rolls back and parries the hit with his forearm. Note how he is also moving into the side kick.

C: Tackett delivers the side kick to Cunningham's lead leg at the same time he deflects Cunningham's punch.

Covering the High Hook Punch

Once the student has practiced against straight punches and has a good grasp on how to defend against them, it's time to add the high hook punch to the mix. It's important to drill defense against high hooks because they are aimed at the head and can do the most damage.

When defending against a high hook punch, the student needs to make sure of the following things:

- He needs to keep his balance.
- He needs to use his lead hand to smother and prevent the trainer from using the non-attacking rear hand.

- He needs to keep his fingertips at the side of his head so there is some give if the hook punch makes contact with his glove.

He doesn't move his rear shoulder forward when placing the glove at the side of his head. This would allow the high hook to land on the glove with a lot of force. Instead the student should bring his head forward to the glove because he'll have a better chance of being inside the hit. When done correctly, the punch should miss the student entirely. The glove is there for safety; if hit, it will soften the blow.

Like in the other drills, the trainer will attack with the high hook while the student responds with the appropriate technique. Start stationary and then add footwork. Always begin slowly before adding speed and movement. In the Wednesday Night Group, we practice defending against high hooks a lot because they can cause a lot of damage. So be careful!

Cover Against the High Hook

A: Tim Tackett and Patrick Cunningham face each other in fighting stances at close range.

B: Cunningham throws a hook punch.

C: Tackett twists his body forward to the right. He puts more weight on his lead leg to twist his rear foot clockwise. This gets him inside the hook. At the same time, he covers Cunningham with his lead glove.

Simultaneous Parry and Hit

A: Cunningham and Tackett face each other in fighting stances.

B: When Tackett senses Cunningham's preparation for a high hook, he immediately begins to parry with his rear hand.

C: By putting weight on his lead leg, Tackett also simultaneously hits. Learn more about simultaneous-block-and-hit drills on page 78 of Volume 1.

Beat-to-the-Punch Drill

A: Once Tackett is proficient at the simultaneous parry and hit, he will practice intercepting Cunningham's hook before it makes contact with his covering glove. In effect, Tackett will drill stop-hitting Cunningham's punch.

B: As soon as Tackett is aware of Cunningham's intention, he stop-hits the punch with a straight lead.

C: Tackett wants to hit Cunningham before Cunningham hits Tackett's focus glove. This is why Tackett must use this drill to really practice his awareness and speed.

Catching and Rolling Against Combination Attacks

When you are able to defend against a straight lead punch, straight rear punch and hook punch with ease, you can start defending against these punches in various combinations. The combinations can include any hand tool. For example:

- The trainer does a 1 – 2 combination, and the student catches the straight lead punch and shoulder-rolls or catches the straight rear punch.
- The trainer does a 1 – 3 combination, and the student catches the straight lead punch and covers the hook.
- The trainer does a 1 – 3 – 2 combination, and the student catches the straight lead punch, covers the hook, and shoulder-rolls or catches the straight rear punch.
- The trainer does a 1 – 2 – 3 combination, and the student catches the straight lead punch, shoulder-rolls or catches the straight rear punch and covers the hook.
- Remember that in boxing, 1 refers to a jab or straight lead, 2 refers to a straight rear punch, and 3 refers to a lead high hook punch.

When you start defending against these combination attacks, make sure that whoever is acting as the trainer starts by punching slowly, doesn't hit hard and attacks with a steady rhythm. Once you feel comfortable, the trainer can pick up the pace and power.

Against the Double Jab

A: Patrick Cunningham jabs at Tim Tackett. Tackett catches the jab with the palm of his glove.

B: They are both stationary during this drill, but as Tackett improves, they could start moving around with footwork before Cunningham jabs.

C: When moving, Cunningham would try to hit Tackett when he is off-balance. This would help Tackett learn to move with stability.

Against a 1 – 2 Combination

A: Tackett catches a jab, which is the first punch in a 1 – 2 combination.

B: He then rolls his shoulder to parry Cunningham's follow-up straight rear punch.

C: Of course, Tackett could also use distance to avoid the straight rear punch.

Against a Three-Punch Combination

A: Tackett catches a straight lead punch.

B: Tackett fades back by rolling his shoulder against Cunningham's straight rear punch.

C: Tackett then covers against Cunningham's front-hand high hook.

Attacking With Combinations After the Catch

Work on different follow-ups to the catch drills. If you have to catch, shoulder-roll or cover, you should return fire as soon as you are able to—preferably before your opponent can fire another attack. For example, once you have caught a punch with your rear glove, you can then fire a straight lead to a front hook to a straight rear punch. In boxing terminology, this would be a 1 – 3 – 2 combination. Some of the other combination follow-up punches or other attacks you can use are as follows:

- straight rear – hook – straight rear
- 3 – 2 – 3
- overhead – uppercut – overhead
- high to low punches
- low to high punches
- elbows and/or knees
- any straight blast
- shove to kicks
- clinches
- takedowns
- add your own

When working with a list like this, the Wednesday Night Group spends time on one before moving on to the next item. It might be helpful to make a poster and hang it on the wall or give a copy to each practitioner. Practitioners then pair up as student and trainer and take turns going through the list. Generally, they will only have time to thoroughly go through the first three or four combinations on the list. When the Wednesday Night Group meets again, that student-trainer pair will review the ones they practiced last time before moving on to the next items. Note: When practitioners get the list, they should be familiar with all the techniques listed.

Eventually, you'll want to train against the listed combinations with broken rhythm. Learn more about broken rhythm on pages 110-112 of Volume 1.

To hit with broken rhythm, the trainer can attack as follows:

- hit – pause – hit – hit
- hit – hit – pause – hit
- slow – fast – fast
- fast – slow – fast

The final move in any broken-rhythm attack is always done as fast and hard as is necessary to accomplish what is needed in the circumstance.

Drills like this will stop the student from trying to think ahead to what might be coming because he must relate to a broken-rhythm attack. He is no longer able to count on defending against a steady-rhythm attack.

Defending Against Combination Attacks

You also want to be able to defend against combination attacks after you catch. For example, you may catch an opponent's jab, but he might follow-up with another jab or hand tool before you have time to counterattack.

Like in other drills, start stationary. When the student can catch and defend against combination attacks from a stationary position, he and the trainer can start adding footwork. In a moving situation, the trainer would try to hit the student when he is in motion and possibly off-balance. This teaches the student how to defend against attacks while moving.

Defending Against the Double Jab

A: Patrick Cunningham and Tim Tackett stand at the fighting measure.

B: Cunningham attempts to jab Tackett's chin, but Tackett catches the strike in his glove.

C, D: Cunningham then jabs again, and Tackett catches it again.

Defending Against the Jab With Sliding Leverage

A: When Cunningham jabs, Tackett cross-parries with sliding leverage.

Defending Against a 1 – 2 Combination (Straight Lead to Straight Rear Punch) No. 1

A: Cunningham launches a straight lead punch, which Tackett catches.

B: When Cunningham follows up with a straight rear punch, Tackett defends with a shoulder roll.

Defending Against a 1 – 2 Combination No. 2

A: Cunningham and Tackett continue their combination practice.

B: Cunningham attacks with a straight lead punch, which Tackett catches.

C: Cunningham attacks again with a straight rear punch, but this time Tackett uses distance to defend.

Safety Boxing Against Unmatched Lead Attacks

While you can use the catch with the rear hand against the jab or straight lead, there are some specialized defenses for unmatched leads. The drills in this section are more in keeping with the JKD principles of hitting into the attack and are less passive.

Sliding Leverage Against a Straight Lead

A: Patrick Cunningham attempts to hit Tim Tackett with a lead jab from an unmatched stance.

B: Tackett counters it with a vertical-fist sliding-leverage punch. He does this by moving off the line—sliding across it—while simultaneously punching into the strike. Learn more about sliding leverage on pages 84-86 of Volume 1.

Cross Parry

A: Cunningham tries to hit Tackett from an unmatched stance.

B: Tackett cross-parries the jab and uses sliding leverage to hit Cunningham in the face.

Parry Against the Left Hook

A: Cunningham and Tackett face each other in unmatched stances.

B: Tackett parries the strike by cutting into the tool.

C: He hooks inside Cunningham's strike with a vertical hook. Learn a similar technique on page 86 of Volume 1.

Counters to Shovel Hooks

The shovel hook is one of the basic infighting tools in Western boxing. Since it is used to great effect, the Wednesday Night Group spends a lot of time learning how to do it well and defend against it properly. Learn more about the shovel hook on page 52 of Volume 1.

The Wednesday Night Group addresses the drills shown in the pictures below one defense at a time. When the student can do them all, the trainer can then attack repeatedly with the shovel hook while the student flows from one defense to another. Eventually, the student should try to punch before the attacker has time to deliver a second hit.

Rear-Forearm Block

A: Jeremy Lynch and Vince Raimondi (right) face each other in fighting stances.

B: Lynch attacks with a front shovel hook, which Raimondi blocks. To block the hit, Raimondi twists to the right and drops his rear forearm.

Front Sliding-Leverage Block and Hit

A: Lynch attacks with a rear shovel hook. Notice how Raimondi is already moving into action.

B: Raimondi blocks the hit. At the same time, Raimondi uses his blocking arm to hit with an uppercut, cutting into Lynch's punch.

Scoop Parry and Hit

A: Raimondi executes a scoop parry against Lynch's front shovel hook. In the scoop parry, Raimondi scoops Lynch's arm at the elbow, deflecting the hit so it passes his body without making contact.

B: Raimondi then keeps control of Lynch's elbow. Since Raimondi has both controlled Lynch's elbow and opened Lynch's side up, it is easy for him to strike Lynch with his own shovel hook.

Rear Scoop Parry and Hit

A: This time Raimondi scoop-parries Lynch's rear uppercut with his rear arm.

B: He then strikes Lynch with a front shovel hook to the inside of Lynch's arm. He could just as easily hit Lynch in the chin with an uppercut on the same line.

Scoop Parry to an Uppercut on the Inside Line

A: Like the previous sequence, Raimondi scoop-parries Lynch.

B: This time Raimondi hits Lynch with an uppercut to the chin on the same line.

Shovel-Hook Flow Drill

A: When Raimondi has mastered all of the previously shown defenses, he can do the shovel-hook flow drill. He and Lynch are in fighting stances.

B, C: Lynch hits low with a shovel hook. Raimondi drops his elbow to block.

D, E: Lynch hits low with a shovel hook. Raimondi counters with a forearm block that becomes an uppercut to Lynch's chin.

F, G, H: Lynch hits low with a shovel hook. Raimondi then scoops and returns a rear shovel hook.

I, J: Lynch hits low with a shovel hook. Raimondi scoops the punch and hits with an uppercut.

Slip Drills

Slip drills come directly from boxing and help you learn to slip inside your opponent's punch. Slipping helps you get into position to either take an opponent to the ground or get in close enough to execute boxing punches. For these reasons, it's important to slip at the last second. If you slip too soon, your opponent will just change his attack to hit you, and at that moment, you are vulnerable.

One of the best ways to practice slipping is to have your partner try to hit you with a boxing glove on his hand. The advantage of this is that the trainer can really try to hit you, which makes the drill more realistic. The disadvantage is that because of the size of the boxing glove, you have to exaggerate the distance of the slip. In reality, the best distance for a slip is close enough so that the punch grazes your ear. The less you have to slip, the more your stance will be in balance and the quicker you can hit with a counterattack.

After practicing with a boxing glove, the student and trainer can do a variation of a slip drill. Practice it with a bare-hand palm hit to the forehead; the student slips the head strike. Or the student and trainer can practice with an MMA-type glove. The trainer can hit with either a high straight lead or a rear punch so the student can practice slipping to the inside and outside line. After that, the student would work on slipping the straight rear punch. Following practice against the straight lead and rear punches, the trainer can then start throwing combinations to the inside or outside. Following up that practice, the student and trainer will practice bobbing and weaving against high hooks. There are also drills available for the trainer to learn to counter a slip.

Also note that the student can stand with his hands behind his back because doing so will force him to slip; he won't be able to cover or block.

Slip Drill

A: Dennis Blue (right) and Patrick Cunningham face each other. Blue is the student and has his hands behind his back to make sure he slips.

B: When Cunningham hits with a high straight lead, Blue begins to slip.

C: He slips to the inside.

D, E: Blue could also slip to the outside. Note that Blue slips at least to the attacker's elbow so that Cunningham can't counter the slip.

Slip Drill With a Delayed Hit

A: To make sure that Blue slips at the last possible moment, Cunningham will punch with a delayed hit.

B: He begins his strike but briefly stops.

C: Then he executes it fully. If Blue slipped during the delayed hit, Cunningham could have followed his movement and countered him.

Slip Against the Straight Rear Punch

A: Blue stands with his hands behind his back and faces Cunningham.

B: When Cunningham throws a straight rear punch, Blue slips to the outside.

Bobbing and Weaving Against a High Hook

A, B: Blue bobs Cunningham's hook.

C, D: Blue weaves under and to the outside of Cunningham's second hook. Blue ends up in the same place he started.

Countering a Slip

A: Jeremy Lynch (right) faces Dennis Blue. Note that Blue is wearing Thai pads for protection.

B: Lynch throws a straight lead punch, which Blue counters by slipping to the outside.

C: Lynch counters by kneeing the pads with his rear knee.

D: Blue then gives Lynch a visual cue by holding up the Thai pad. Lynch hits the pad with a hook punch.

Stop-Hit and Stop-Kick

One of the most effective ways to deal with a kick is to move forward and intercept it with a punch while the attacker is off-balance and standing on one leg. The hardest thing to learn is when it is safe to move forward and to do so with the proper speed and timing. Stop-hits won't work if you don't close the distance fast and deep enough because the attacker's leg will not be extended or have any momentum behind his strike.

The stop-kick is the same as the stop-hit but instead of punching, you intercept an attack with a kick. In jeet kune do, the three most prevalent stop-kicks are the side kick, the leg obstruction and the jam. Learn more about the leg obstruction on pages 149-152 of Volume 1.

To practice stop-hitting and stop-kicking, the trainer will throw kicks at the student and the student will defend against them, first with distance. Instead of trying to stop-hit, the student wants to observe the trainer's preparation. Later, the student will either use distance for defense or he will use speed and proper timing to get in a stop-hit.

Note: Whenever you aren't sure what kick the opponent is using or if you're too late to stop-hit, stop-kick or jam, use distance and then counterattack. Otherwise, if you hesitate at all, the old adage "he who hesitates is lost" applies and you will be kicked.

Stop-Hit

A: Jeremy Lynch (left) and Dennis Blue face each other.

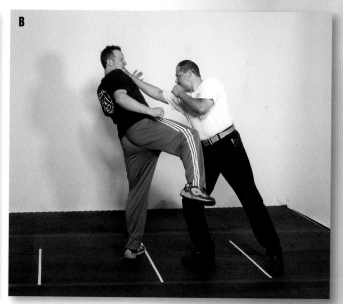

B: Lynch slides up to kick Blue. Because Blue has the timing right, he stop-hits him with a straight lead punch.

Stop-Kick

A: Lynch is going to try to kick Blue.

B: Because Blue noticed his preparation, he stop-kicks Lynch with a leg obstruction.

Using Distance

A: Blue and Lynch face each other in standing positions.

B: Lynch side-kicks, but Blue wasn't sure about the attack. He moves back with a push-step or slide.

C: If Blue did stop-hit, he would have done it before Lynch's kicking foot hit the ground or before Lynch recovered to the fighting measure.

Using Distance to Stop-Hit

A: If your awareness is slow, you can purposely move back to draw a second kick, then you'll have time to stop-hit. Here, Blue will do that against Lynch.

B: Lynch slides forward to kick, but Blue moves back.

C: Lynch attempts to slide forward with a kick again.

D: This time, Blue push-steps forward to stop-hit Lynch. Notice that Blue has moved inside the kick so it doesn't land with power.

Angle and Stop-Hit

A: Blue could also angle for a stop-hit.

B: When Lynch moves in to kick, Blue curves to the right.

C: By moving off the centerline, Blue is inside Lynch's kick and has room to stop-hit. Learn more about angling on pages 98-99 of Volume 1.

Countering the Stop-Kick

Anytime you attack, you are vulnerable to an opponent's stop-hit or stop-kick. At the same time, you can use a stop-hit or stop-kick to intercept an opponent's attack. Against an opponent who can stop-hit with skill, it's difficult to land any hand attack without running into a stop-kick. In jeet kune do, this is called "offensive defense." If your opponent is the type of fighter who either tries to block your attack or run from it, you do not need to worry about a possible stop-kick. But you can't be sure what kind of fighter an unfamiliar opponent is, so it's safer to assume he can control distance and will use a stop-kick if you try to use a hand attack. To avoid the stop-kick as you bridge the gap, you can use a low shin/knee side kick, the leg obstruction, the leg lift or even the jam. Learn more about these techniques in Volume 1: stop-hits on page 79, stop-kicks on pages 95-97, the jam on pages 97-98 and the leg obstruction on pages 149-152.

The side kick is the most powerful of the kicks used to attack the opponent's lead leg in order to avoid his stop-hit or stop-kick. However, because the kick requires you to be sideways to your target, the transition to a hand attack is not as fast as with the leg lift or leg obstruction.

In regards to the leg lift, many of the JKD practitioners in the Wednesday Night Group find it very valuable and use it a lot. The leg lift is the fastest way to transition to a hand attack because the kick comes straight up from the floor with no counter-rotation of the body. At the same time, it is also the weakest kick of the three because there is no hip torque to give it power. To do it, you simply bring your leg straight up from the floor as you slide up to bridge the gap and hit the opponent's shin with it. While it does not have a lot of force, the leg lift will prevent the opponent from using his front leg to stop-kick you. What you are doing is blocking his kick. From here, transitioning to a hand attack is very easy and fast because you don't have to adjust your body to strike with your lead hand. The leg lift should be enough of a distraction that you can deliver a hand attack like the finger jab before the opponent knows what is going on.

The leg obstruction is probably the most used by the JKD practitioners in the Wednesday Night Group. It starts just like the leg lift, but as you slide up, you rotate your body to the right and slam your leg into your opponent's shin. While it looks similar to the leg lift, you lean further back in the leg obstruction so that the transition to a hand attack is slightly slower, but the power in the kick is greater. While the leg obstruction is not as strong as the side kick, the transition to a hand attack is much faster.

When drilling with a trainer, he will try to stop-kick you when you advance. If he uses a shin/knee side kick, then he is using the JKD principle of attacking with the longest weapon (side kick) against the closest target (your lead leg). Begin by practicing the shin/knee side kick, leg obstruction and leg lift from a stationary position at the fighting measure. After practicing all three, you'll probably find one feels most natural to you, but you should practice all three because they will intercept an opponent's stop-kick. Practice all three kicks so that you can move forward fast enough and without preparation so the trainer can't stop-kick. Because each kick will make contact with the trainer's shin, he should wear a shin guard; that way the student can practice with some force. In fact, any leg obstruction should hit with enough force so that the trainer's awareness concentrates on his lead leg, giving you enough time to follow through with a hand attack. He won't know what's happening and won't be able to stop-hit you.

Once you have practiced all kicks from a stationary position and without the trainer reacting to your attack, the trainer can start trying to stop-kick your advances. If done fast enough and with little preparation, you should still be able to obstruct the stop-kick before it gets too far off the ground. If you are beyond the fighting measure when you attack, the trainer will be able to obstruct your own leg obstruction and score with his own hand attack. That's why understanding and controlling distance is so important in JKD.

From there, you can make the drill even more difficult: You and the trainer both get to move and try to obstruct intercepting attacks.

Side Kick to a Finger Jab

A: Dennis Blue (right) and Patrick Cunningham are in fighting stances, facing each other.

B: Blue wants to attack Cunningham with a finger jab, but he knows Cunningham will stop-hit him. So Blue stop-kicks Cunningham with a side kick.

C: Blue then attacks with a finger jab. Note: The side kick leaves Blue far away from Cunningham, but the kick should have been so strong that the damage to Cunningham's leg is great and gives Blue enough time to land a hand attack. If Blue does not feel that he has enough time to deliver a hand attack, he can always pendulum back to the fighting measure and assess the situation. Learn more about the pendulum on page 63 of Volume 1.

Leg Lift Against a Stop-Kick

A: Cunningham and Blue face each other in fighting stances.

B: Blue brings his leg straight up from the floor to make contact with Cunningham's shin. Note: All Blue wants to do is prevent Cunningham from stop-kicking him. The leg lift accomplishes that.

C: From there, Blue quickly transitions into a finger jab. While this is the least powerful of all the stop-kick counters, it is the fastest transition to the finger jab because you don't have to rotate your body much.

Leg Obstruction

A: Dennis Blue stops Jeremy Lynch's lead punch with a leg obstruction. Notice that Blue covers Lynch's attacking hand as a safety measure and at the same time has his lead hand next to his chin, ready to launch a hand attack.

B: In this leg obstruction, Dennis Blue does a leg obstruction on Patrick Cunningham from the opposite side. Notice how much further Blue is leaning back than in the leg lift.

The Jam

The jam is one of the lesser-known but most effective defenses in the JKD arsenal. In a jam, you literally jam into your opponent, preventing him from doing any type of counterattack. Learn more about the jam on pages 96-98 of Volume 1.

To jam, you need to throw yourself at your opponent with great force and speed. That's why jamming practice usually involves a kicking shield first. After the student has practiced some, he can try it against his trainer's kick. The trainer holds the kicking shield and faces the student, as if the student were going to side-kick. The trainer steps forward, and the student throws a jam as fast and hard as he can into the shield.

Note: Because the jam works so well, it tends to knock the trainer down. Of course, this only happens when the student does the jam with proper power. In the Wednesday Night Group, we need to tell practitioners not to jam while sparring. No one wants to attack a person who can jam with both speed and force.

(For further reference, *Bruce Lee's Fighting Method* has a great example of how to do a jam.)

Jam With Kicking Shield

A

B

A: Dennis Blue (left) faces Jeremy Lynch, who is holding a kicking shield.

B: When Lynch steps forward, Blue jams forward as hard and fast as he can.

Jam Without Kicking Shield

A: Lynch and Blue face each other in fighting stances.

B: When Lynch starts to kick, Blue throws his body into the kick to jam it.

Jam Drill With Variation

A: Once the student can do the jam without hesitation, the trainer can vary his attacks. Here, Blue and Lynch face each other in fighting stances.

B: Lynch attacks with a hand tool instead.

C, D: Blue then jams Lynch's attack.

Defense Against Rear-Leg Thai Roundhouse Kick

Because of the prevalence of MMA training, the rear-leg Thai-style kick is very popular, so effort should be made to make sure you can defend against it. In jeet kune do, we call that type of kick a hook kick because it follows the same line as a hook punch. Many other arts call that same kick a roundhouse kick. Whatever you name it, it's a powerful kick, and care must be taken when you try and block it. The kick's contact is with the shin rather than the foot. The closer the kick lands to the targeted shin's foot, the more power the kick has. In contrast, the closer the kick lands to the targeted shin's knee, the less power it has. Practice all the defenses below with care. Make sure you start slow and then pick up the speed.

Angle and Catching the Kick

A: Dennis Blue and Jeremy Lynch face each other in fighting stances.

B: Lynch executes a hook kick.

C: As Lynch kicks, Blue angles away and to the left of the strike's power. This movement puts Blue closer to Lynch's knee.

D: Now Blue can wrap his lead hand around Lynch's knee. He slaps the kick at the knee to diffuse its power. From here, Blue can throw Lynch by kicking his leg out from under him. Note: This technique requires great timing. Make sure you start working on it slowly and carefully. Take time to build up to full speed and power.

Cut Kick

A: One of the best ways to deal with a Thai roundhouse is to take a technique from Thai boxing: attack the opponent's supporting leg, which is what Patrick Cunningham and Dennis Blue will practice. They will need great timing and a lot of practice to do it correctly. Cunningham and Blue square off at the fighting measure.

B: As Cunningham takes a slight step forward to kick with his rear leg, Blue angles away from the force of the kick and does a front-leg hook kick to Cunningham's supporting leg.

C: To continue the drill, Cunningham could step up with his rear leg or slide up and kick with his lead leg. Blue would then have to read the kick and angle away from it to cut-kick. Blue would use his rear leg to cut-kick if Cunningham slid up to hook-kick with his lead leg.

Stop-Hitting a Hook Kick

A: Lynch starts his hook kick by taking a lead step forward.

B: Blue stop-hits with a straight lead to the chest. Note: To practice the stop-hit with enough power so the kick doesn't land, the trainer should hold a Thai pad on his chest. Also, if Lynch were in a left lead, Blue would take a slight lead step to his right and stop-hit with a straight rear punch.

Defensive Focus-Glove Drills

Defensive focus-glove drills are a great method of practicing defense and counter-punching at the same time. The way it works is that the trainer uses one of the focus gloves to hit the student. The student then defends and returns a counterattack to the focus gloves. Once the student has worked on a few of these exchanges, the trainer will throw one of them at random while the student defends and returns fire. You should work your way up to being able to defend against any attack with the focus glove. It takes skill and practice to be able to feed the gloves properly. Here are some other variations:

- The trainer feeds a hit on another line.
- The student punches first, and the trainer responds with the glove, helping the student move from attack to defense for reaction training.
- The student knows what the attack will be and will react with the proper response.
- The student doesn't know which of two or three specific attacks will occur.
- The student doesn't know which counterattack the trainer will feed him.
- The trainer hits with one or two strikes while the student slips in or out and/or hits.
- The trainer and student can add kicks.
- The trainer can mix any of the above.

The trainer and student can also see how many left-against-right drills they can come up with or add boxing combinations and straight blasts as follow-ups. However, when the student can do the drills from a stationary stance with proper reaction timing, the trainer should vary his attack with footwork and broken rhythm.

As you can see, there are lots of possibilities. You can come up with many more. This will add variety to training and keep the student and trainer's interest up while they are improving their defense, hitting and reaction time.

Jab or Hook With Glove

A: Vince Raimondi (left) and Tim Tackett Jr. practice with focus gloves.

B: Tackett Jr. strikes vertically at Raimondi with the front focus glove. He could throw a hook, jab or straight lead punch. Raimondi does a simultaneous block and hit as a response. He could also have stop-hit the strike.

Straight Rear Punch With Glove

A: Raimondi and Tackett Jr. continue working on focus-glove drills.

B: Tackett Jr. attacks with a straight rear punch. Raimondi responds with a shoulder roll.

C: Raimondi returns a rear uppercut to the front glove. Note: Tackett Jr. must be quick in his placement of the glove for Raimondi's counterattack.

Counter to Low Jab

A: Raimondi and Tackett Jr. face each other at the fighting measure.

B: Raimondi steps forward to strike with a straight lead punch.

C: Tackett Jr. counters with a low straight lead punch on the lead focus glove. At the same time, Raimondi defends against it by lowering his rear elbow.

D: He hits the rear glove again with a straight lead punch.

E: Raimondi could also have returned a straight rear punch.

Inside Slip to Straight Rear Punch

A: Raimondi and Tackett Jr. face each other in fighting stances. Tackett Jr. is still the trainer.

B: When Tackett Jr. attempts to hit Raimondi with his lead focus glove, Raimondi slips to the inside and does a simultaneous counter with a straight rear punch.

Bob and Weave Against Front Hook

A: Raimondi and Tackett Jr. face each other in fighting stances.

B: When Tackett Jr. executes a front hook, Raimondi bobs and weaves under it to hit with a lead uppercut.

C: Raimondi follows the uppercut with a straight rear punch.

Elbow Cover Against Low Front Hook

A: Raimondi and Tackett Jr. square off at close range.

B: Tackett Jr. hits to Raimondi's left side with his right focus glove. Raimondi then lowers his body and covers his side with his elbow. In a real fight, someone who punches to the body with a bare fist and runs into an elbow risks a broken hand.

C; Raimondi then hits the focus glove with a front uppercut.

D: Raimondi immediately follows up with a rear uppercut to the same focus glove. This drill teaches a student to go from defense to offense when at close range. The trainer must be careful to feed the focus gloves correctly.

Focus-Glove Drill With Kicks

A: Raimondi and Tackett Jr. face each other in fighting stances. Tackett Jr. is the trainer and holds focus gloves.

B: Tackett Jr. throws a jab, but Raimondi catches it.

C: Tackett Jr. follows up with a side kick, although he could also do a front or hook kick. Raimondi defends with distance.

D: Raimondi counters with a hook kick to the focus glove. Note that Tackett Jr. must move his glove into a visual cue quickly so Raimondi knows what to kick with.

———cᴧᴈ———

There are lots of drills and training methods in this chapter. I don't recommend that you take, for example, the drills or training methods in one chapter and spend weeks going through each one at the exclusion of the other drills in this chapter. In the Wednesday Night Group, we like to begin with the basic stance and work our way through techniques like the straight lead punch; we practice while stationary first and then while moving. Once the student knows how to do that, we work on how to defend against it. At the same time, we may also be working on one of the basic kicks in the same manner.

The training methods in each section are listed in the order in which we usually work on them. In the same lesson, we might work on the catch against the straight lead punch or jab, using distance against a side kick, and a defensive focus-glove drill.

Chapter 6
ATTACKS

There are three aspects to any attack. They are:

- accuracy
- speed
- power

Accuracy refers to hitting the exact spot you aim for and at the correct distance. Speed refers to the amount of time you need to hit the target before your opponent can react to it. Power refers to the force you must generate to achieve your objective.

In this chapter, you will learn various training methods, principles and drills to hone your attacking skills. At the Wednesday Night Group, we generally work on the drills in this chapter concurrently with the defensive drills in Chapter 5. This chapter also deals with the five ways of attack in jeet kune do. While Volume 1 had an entire chapter devoted to trapping, this volume will show all five ways in a single chapter. It would probably be a good idea to review Chapters 6 and 7 in Volume 1 because many of the concepts are relevant to the drills in this chapter.

Training Tips

This section lists general attack tips that we practice at the Wednesday Night Group. First, before any attack, stay loose and poised. Second, when striking, have an economical start with no preparation. It should be one continuous movement and end with exploding force. Third, during the attack, you should travel on the most direct line to the target. Also make sure you have as much defensive covering as possible because any attack will leave a line open for your opponent to counterattack. After the attack, you need to recover back to the fighting measure or continue the attack. Lastly, always keep balance before, during and after the attack.

Single Direct Attacks and Single Angular Attacks

The first way of attack is a singular one in that only one tool is used to attack an opponent. Single direct attacks, or SDAs, are executed on a direct line to the target, regardless of whether the line is straight or curved. SDAs are sometimes referred to as "simple" attacks. An example of an SDA is the straight lead punch.

A subcategory of the first way of attack is the single angular attack. It is the same as an SDA except that you attack at an angle instead of directly toward the opponent. Two examples of SAAs are the curved right straight lead punch and the curved right side kick. Learn more about these attacks on pages 42-43 and 63 of Volume 1. If you've been reading the other chapters in this book, you've probably already picked up how the drills in Chapters 3, 4 and 5 are based on SDAs and SAAs. For example, the trainer could give the student a visual cue so the student responds with a direct or angular hand or kicking attack. Note: While the hook kick may look like an SAA, it is considered to be an SDA because it strikes at a target on one line.

Single Direct Attack With a Hand Attack

A

B

A: Tim Tackett Jr. (left) and Dennis Blue square off in fighting stances.

B: Tackett Jr. hits Blue with a straight lead punch. This is an attack that follows a direct line with no deviation.

Single Direct Attack With Hook Kick

A: Tackett Jr. and Blue face each other in fighting stances. This time Blue is the student.

B: Blue executes his hook kick.

C: When Blue executes his hook kick, trainer Tackett Jr. covers to protect himself. Note: Covering is a passive move, and covering a full-power kick may injure your arms. When starting training, it's a good idea to have some kind of protection in case the student loses control. Once the student can kick the focus glove with skill and control, you should no longer practice this way. In combat, your hands would be in the same position as Tackett Jr's, but instead you would have stepped forward and intercepted the hook kick with a stop-hit.

Single Angular Attack: Curved Right Straight Lead Punch

A: Tackett Jr. and Blue face each other in fighting stances.

B: Tackett Jr. curves right and attacks Blue with a straight lead punch.

Attack by Combination

The second way of attack is an attack by combination. ABCs are defined as two or more continuous single or angular attacks with a steady or broken rhythm. Some examples of ABCs are hand to hand, or hitting with any two hand attacks; hand to foot, or hitting first with a hand attack and following up with a kicking tool; foot to hand, or hitting first with a kicking tool and following up with a hand attack; and foot to foot, or hitting with any two kicking tools.

Here is a simple overview of common attacks by combinations. Note that H stands for "hand" and F stands for "foot." In the Wednesday Night Group, we use the following as a checklist in our training:

- H – H – H
- H – H – F
- H – F – H
- H – F – F
- F – H – F
- F – H – H
- F – F – H
- F – F – F

In our garage, we have this list of attacks by combination on a poster on the wall, and students are given a specific amount of time to go through this list whereby they create their own combination, or they may be given a specific combination to work from. For example, an F – F – H could be low side kick followed by another side kick to a straight lead punch.

Another guide we use is the following list:

- high straight lead to low hook kick to high straight lead
- high straight lead to low inverted kick to high straight lead
- high straight lead to low side kick to high straight lead
- high straight lead to any low kick to high straight lead
- high lead to low lead to high lead
- high lead to low straight rear to high straight lead
- any high hand to any low hand to any high hand
- any low kick to any high punch
- any low kick to any high kick
- any hand to any foot
- any hand to any hand
- any foot to any hand
- any foot to any foot

In training this list, the Wednesday Night Group begins by doing all of the above from a stationary position. From there, start adding movement wherein the trainer and/or student moves forward. Then practice the techniques by moving backward. After mastering that, add elbows and knee strikes as part of an ABC; for example, you and your trainer can do a kick-to-punch-to-elbow combination. Eventually, you'll practice ABCs with light sparring, wherein the trainer attacks while the student defends or vice versa.

After doing that, you and your partner should do two-man drills wherein the trainer does a combination attack and the student uses distance to avoid it; the student then returns the same attack, or vice versa. This particular drill allows the partner being attacked to learn to observe his partner's preparation and recognize the kind of attack, and then to show that by returning.

Of course, once you've practiced all these variations, feel free to add your own.

Angle-and-Kick Drill

A: Jeremy Lynch holds two Thai pads for Dennis Blue.

B: Blue angles to the right.

C: He angles back in to execute a controlled hook kick to Lynch's front leg.

D,E: He then does a left and right hook kick to the pads.

Attack by Combination With Broken Rhythm

Once you've worked on the basic principles and techniques for ABCs, try to take the hit combinations discussed in the section above and work on them with broken rhythm. Broken rhythm means you change up the cadence of your attack by altering the time between strikes or changing up your strikes' speeds. Doing so makes it more difficult for an opponent to predict your next movement. Learn more about broken rhythm on pages 110-112 of Volume 1.

Broken rhythm can also break up your opponent's defensive rhythm. For example, if you attack in a steady rhythm, your opponent can anticipate your next attack and react on preparation. When you use broken rhythm, your opponent can't read your next move. He gets confused and loses his own cadence, making him vulnerable to attack.

One way to work on broken rhythm is to take the combination techniques in this book and do them in the examples below. You can do this by yourself at first, either stationary or while shadow boxing. From there, come up with drills whereby you practice attacking with broken rhythm while the trainer defends against it. You can use the same methodology as discussed in the earlier ABC section:

- Practice it stationary with a partner.
- Practice it while moving forward with any kicking or hand tools.
- Practice it moving backward on each technique.
- Add elbows and knees to the ABC.
- Do all of the above with a partner in light sparring.
- Add your own.

Note: With broken rhythm, it is obviously not feasible to do a two-man mirror drill.

Many of the drills in the other parts of this book can also be adapted to practice broken-rhythm attacks by combination.

The following are examples of broken-rhythm combinations:

- H – H – pause – H, as in straight lead – straight rear – pause – hook. (Steady rhythm would be hit – hit – hit.)
- H – pause – H – H, as in straight lead – pause – straight rear – hook.

You can also use pace to break up your rhythm. Slow down the pace of one or two hits. For example:

- fast – slow – fast
- slow – fast – fast
- slow – slow – fast

Progressive Indirect Attack

The third way of attack is the progressive indirect attack. A PIA is a great attack if your opponent blocks or uses distance against your attack. The PIA starts with a feint and is followed by a single or combination attack; basically you follow up with an SDA, SAA or ABC. The two main purposes of a PIA are: (a) to overcome an opponent whose defense is strong and fast enough to deal with a direct attack, and (b) to offer variation in your pattern of attack.

When you feint, your opponent will move to block or parry the attack. But the "indirect" in a PIA means you don't want to wait for the block. Your strike should keep ahead of the block but prolong the feint long enough that your opponent doesn't have time to react. You can also think of it this way: The feint shortens the distance to your target by half; this means you only have to travel the last half with your strike.

You do need to be aware of what kind of opponent you are facing to use a PIA. Learn more about opponent identification on page 105 of Volume 1. If your opponent is a blocker, you can use the PIA to open a line of attack for the opponent and switch to another line halfway. If your opponent is a runner, you can usually catch him while he is moving back by stealing a step and then using a kicking or hand tool. If your opponent is a banger, you probably shouldn't use the PIA; the opponent is just going to run at you, and a fake or feint won't deter him. If your opponent is an interceptor, like a JKD practitioner, then a PIA probably won't work because the opponent will stop-hit or stop-kick; he will simply hit anyone who fakes or feints.

Like with the other ways of attack, there are basic PIA combinations in steady and broken rhythm:

- foot feint to hand attack
- hand feint to foot attack
- high-line feint to low-line attack
- high-line feint to middle-line attack
- high-line feint to high-line attack
- low-line feint to high-line attack
- low-line feint to middle-line attack
- middle-line feint to high-line attack
- middle-line feint to low-line attack
- inside-line feint to outside-line attack
- outside-line feint to inside-line attack

The most common PIA combinations are on low-to-high, high-to-low, inside-to-outside and outside-to-inside lines.

As mentioned earlier, use this list to train with a partner. Have the designated student throw a PIA at the trainer, who must defend himself. JKD practitioners can eventually go from stationary positions to drills that add footwork or that follow up the PIA with traps. Also work on feinting or faking after a counter. For example, the trainer attacks and the student blocks the attack, then moves into a PIA, such as a low feint and a high hit. Note: A good way to practice feinting is for the trainer to drop an arm for a block. The student then has to learn to react quickly to take advantage of the open line.

Always begin slowly before adding speed and power.

Hand-to-Foot PIA

A: Tim Tackett Jr. and Dennis Blue (right) face each other in fighting stances.

B: Tackett Jr. steals a step forward while feinting with his front hand. Blue is focused on the feint rather than the step and takes a small rear step back.

C: Tackett Jr. takes the opportunity to use a hook kick to close the distance and hit Blue's midsection.

Low-Line Feint to High-Line Strike No. 1

A: Tackett Jr. and Blue continue their PIA practice. This time Blue is the student.

B: Blue fakes a low hook kick to Tackett Jr.'s lead shin.

C: Blue puts his foot down, which brings him close enough to attack with a high-hand strike.

Low-Line Feint to High-Line Strike No. 2

A: Tackett Jr. and Blue continue their PIA practice. Tackett Jr. is now the student.

B: Tackett Jr. feints a low straight lead punch.

C: However, he switches lines unexpectedly with a high hook to Blue's head. Note: In training, of course, you wouldn't actually hit the trainer's head. Always train with control. I've known more than a few guys who have a hard time finding good training partners because they lack control and hurt their fellow practitioners.

Low-Line Feint to High-Line Strike No. 3

A: Tim Tackett (left) faces the trainer.

B: As Tackett feints with a low straight lead punch, the trainer lowers his hand to block it, opening up the upper right side of his body and head.

C: Before the trainer's arm can make contact with the feint, Tackett scores with a backfist when he changes to a high-line attack.

High-Line Feint to Low-Line Hit

A: Tackett (left) faces his trainer.

B: He steps up with a high-line finger jab to the trainer's eyes.

C: But then Tackett switches lines by quickly stepping up with his rear leg to execute a low-line attack to the trainer's groin. Note: In a real conflict, Tackett would then step quickly behind his opponent to avoid an elbow attack.

O.N.E. – 2 Combination

A: Tackett faces his trainer. He is going to use a o.n.e. – 2 combination, which takes advantage of broken rhythm.

B: Tackett does a slow-paced feint. His trainer drops his arm to block it.

C: Tackett executes a swift and powerful hook. Learn more about the o.n.e – 2 combination on pages 111-112 of Volume 1.

Adding Footwork to the PIA

A: Tackett faces his trainer in a fighting stance.

B: He feints a low-line attack. The trainer drops his lead hand to parry the attack.

C: Tackett takes a lead step to execute a straight lead punch.

Progressive Indirect Attacks With Kicks

To make a PIA with a kicking tool effective in combat, you need to make sure of the following things while in training:

- that the feint is deep, sudden and economical.
- that the kicks you select are fast and powerful.
- that the kicks don't deviate too much from the fighting-stance position for fast execution and recovery. In training, you can practice with other kicks.

The techniques in this section are quite difficult and require a lot of training to be effective. Even then, you may never be able to pull some of the PIA kicking attacks in this section in real combat. However, trying them in training will help you work on your flexibility, power and conditioning. And the truth is that if you can do some of these PIA kicking attacks, then the kicking techniques in Chapter 5 will seem much easier.

As in the other section, practice with a partner. Throw PIA attacks at him. Start stationary, then add footwork, then add more complicated elements as mentioned in the other sections. Always start slow before adding speed and power. Remember that the drills in this book don't just improve one aspect at a time. Instead, they focus on many, and such is the case here—dexterity, defense, speed, technique, accuracy, etc.

Front Kick to High Hook Kick

A: Cunningham and Raimondi square off at the fighting measure.

B: Raimondi starts to bridge the gap by sliding up with his rear foot.

C: He then feints with a front kick, which draws Cunningham's low rear-hand block.

D, E: Raimondi takes advantage of the line, which is now open, by hitting with a high hook kick to Cunningham's head. Note: Some of these high kicks can be hard to control. You must make sure not to make any contact with them.

Front Kick to Side Kick

A: Raimondi and Cunningham square off at the fighting measure.

B: Raimondi slides up and feints a low straight kick.

C, D: This time Raimondi scores with a side kick to Cunningham's middle. Note: Raimondi should have enough control to touch his partner's T-shirt and not make contact with his body.

Low-Line Front Kick to High-Line Heel Hook

A: Raimondi and Cunningham square off at the fighting measure.

B, C: After transferring some of his weight to his front leg, Raimondi slides up and feints with a lead straight kick.

D, E: Raimondi then scores with a bent-leg heel hook kick to Cunningham's head. This is all done as one motion. This requires great balance because it is all done by standing on one leg. Learn more about the bent-leg heel hook kick on page 72 of Volume 1.

F, G: Raimondi then returns back to the fighting measure. Note: All this should be done as quickly as possible. Cunningham's job is to stand there and be a target until Raimondi can do the technique while moving and when the trainer tries to defend from a stationary position.

Low Front Kick to High Crescent Kick

A: From the fighting measure, Raimondi slides up to Cunningham.

B, C: He feints a low front kick.

D: Raimondi then throws a clockwise crescent kick.

E: He recovers his stance. Note: Crescent kicks are very hard to control, so make sure your kick misses your partner's head by a good margin. A good way to practice crescent kicks is to throw a front-leg crescent kick followed by a rear-leg crescent kick. You can do this alone, or you can do it with a partner to reference your kick's distance from your partner's head. Learn more about crescent kicks on pages 72-73 of Volume 1.

Crescent-Kick Feint to Crescent-Kick Attack

A, B: Raimondi slides up to Cunningham.

C, D: Raimondi feints as if he is going to throw a clockwise crescent kick.

E: Cunningham moves his head back, reacting to the feint.

F: Raimondi then hops forward and does a counterclockwise crescent kick. Note: Crescent kicks are very hard to control, so make sure your kick misses your partner's head by a good margin.

Continued →

G, H, I, J: After recovering his stance, Raimondi cocks his hip by twisting and then throws a rear-leg crescent kick.

K: Raimondi then recovers his stance. Note: A good way to practice crescent kicks is to practice them as an attack by combination before ever trying them as a PIA attack. To do this practice, throw a front-leg crescent kick followed by a rear-leg crescent kick, like in this picture sequence. You can do this alone, or you can do it with a partner to reference your kick's distance from your partner's head.

High-Kick Feint to Low-Line Side Kick

A: Raimondi and Cunningham face each other in fighting stances.

B: Raimondi slides up to close the distance between him and Cunningham.

C: Raimondi lifts his leg as if he is going to kick high.

D: Instead, he shoots a low side kick to Cunningham's leg. Note: This should all be done in one smooth motion.

High Heel Hook Kick to Middle-Line Hook Kick

A: Raimondi and Cunningham are in fighting stances. They face each other at the fighting measure.

B: Raimondi slides up.

C: He feints a high heel hook kick that misses Cunningham's head.

D, E: Because the miss was intentional, Raimondi is able to change lines and shoot a middle-line hook to Cunningham's midsection.

Crescent-Kick Feint to Spinning Heel Hook Kick

A: Raimondi and Cunningham are in stationary positions, facing each other at the fighting measure.

B, C: Raimondi feints a left rear-leg crescent kick.

D: He then recovers by placing his left foot on the ground and starts to throw a spinning heel hook kick.

E, F: Raimondi does a right-leg heel hook kick to Cunningham's head.

G: Raimondi then recovers his stance. Note: Any crescent kick can be part of an ABC by hitting the opponent's hand to open a line for a second kick.

Crescent-Kick Feint to Spinning Side Kick

A: Raimondi and Cunningham continue their PIA practice with kicks.

B: Raimondi feints a rear-leg crescent kick.

C: He then smoothly changes lines to a side kick that targets Cunningham's midsection.

Kicking Feint to Jumping High-Side Kick

A: After starting in a stationary position, Raimondi slides up to Cunningham; he bridges the gap.

B: Raimondi feints a low kick to Cunningham's leg.

C, D: Then Raimondi jumps up and shoots a high side kick.

Attack by Drawing

The fourth way of attack is an attack by drawing. Attacks by drawing invite an attack by either:

Exposing a part of your body in a way that makes your opponent think he can easily score to the open line. This is the most common method to draw an attack. When using this method, you must be subtle and not obvious. For example, you can drop your arms as if tired, thus giving a logical reason for your arms to be low.

A feint can be used to invite a stop-hit. For example, if you feint low, you may draw a stop-hit, which you can counter. The danger occurs if your opponent stop-kicks instead, so you need to be sure that your opponent's habitual method of intercepting is the stop-hit and not the stop-kick. The method of drawing a stop-hit comes directly from Western fencing, which does not involve kicks. It is important to understand that a certain course of action may not bring the reaction you desire. Always ask yourself the following: "While I'm doing this, what can my opponent do to me?"

Forcing the opponent to counter by purposely trapping one of his limbs while leaving an opening is another version. The idea is that your opponent will take advantage of the opening and attack so you can counter the strike and score a hit.

Some examples on drawing a stop-hit, which you can avoid because you know it's coming, are as follows:

- **Right-to-right example.** Feint a straight rear low punch to draw a front-hook-punch counter. You then bob and weave to a shovel-hook counterattack.
- **Right-to-left example.** Feint a straight lead punch to draw a straight lead stop-hit, which you counter with a cross parry and sliding-leverage straight lead of your own.

The ABD only works when your opponent is not aware you are doing it. It's easier to disguise an ABD attack while moving rather than when you and your trainer are stationary. But in the beginning, start to work on it while stationary, then move on to doing it while in motion. When using footwork, you can (a) retreat to draw the trainer's attack and then counterattack, or (b) advance to draw the trainer's attack and counterattack.

You should try to do a little ABD training in most of your sessions. You can do it in drills in which your partner knows you are drawing his attack as well as in sparring, when he is not aware you are doing an ABD. All in all, it's very easy to make a drill out of any of the examples given in this section. For example, the student can draw an attack by lowering his front or rear arm. And in a reverse of the scenario, the trainer can lower his front or rear arm while the student reacts to the open line.

Lowering the Rear Arm From a Matching Stance

A: Dennis Blue (left) and Jeremy Lynch face off in matching leads.

B: Blue lowers his rear arm, and Lynch takes advantage by attacking with a straight lead punch.

C, D: Blue, however, was drawing the attack, so he counters with a straight rear punch.

Lowering the Lead Arm From a Matching Stance

A, B: Blue lowers his lead arm.

C: Lynch attacks with a straight lead punch.

D: Blue slips inside and counters with a straight rear punch.

Raising the Lead Arm From a Matching Stance

A, B: Blue raises his front arm as if he is going to do a rear-leg hook kick.

C: This draws Lynch's rear punch.

D: Blue parries the attack and, at the same time, scores with a finger jab.

Lowering the Lead Arm From an Unmatched Stance

A, B: Blue lowers his front arm while in an unmatched stance to Lynch.

C, D: Lynch attempts to hit the now-open line with a straight lead attack. Blue counterattacks with a cross parry and sliding-leverage finger jab.

Lowering the Rear Arm From an Unmatched Stance

A, B: Blue lowers his rear arm while in an unmatched stance to Lynch.

C, D: Lynch attacks with a straight rear punch. Blue counters with a cross parry and a straight rear punch of his own.

Drawing a Kick by Lowering the Rear Arm

A: Blue and Lynch face each other at the fighting measure.

B: Blue lowers his rear arm.

C, D: This draws an attempted high hook kick from Lynch to Blue's head.

E: Blue counters by angling to the right while kicking with a low-line hook kick to Lynch's supporting leg.

Drawing a Kick by Raising the Rear Arm, No. 1

A: When you raise an arm, three things will happen: (a) your opponent will do nothing, (b) he will punch to an open line, or (c) he will kick to an open line. In this example, Blue raises his rear arm and sees Lynch's preparation for a kicking attack.

B, C: Seeing an opening, Lynch attacks with a front-leg hook kick. Blue then angles to the right and scores with a straight rear punch.

Drawing a Kick by Raising the Lead Arm, No. 2

A

A: Blue and Lynch continue their ABD practice.

B

B: Blue raises his lead arm.

C: This draws a rear-leg hook kick from Lynch.

D: Blue counters with a stop-hit, knocking Lynch off-balance.

Trapping (Hand-Immobilization Attacks)

The fifth way of attack is known as hand-immobilization attacks or trapping. Trapping goes beyond just trapping an opponent's arm. It also refers to trapping a leg, grabbing hair, etc. In fact, any lock or hold can be considered a trap of some kind.

Most people think of trapping as something you do when someone blocks a punch, but the truth is that it is most effectively done as a counter to an opponent's jab or straight lead punch. For this reason, you want to make sure you keep a tight defense while closing distance, watch out for a stop-hit or stop-kick, be ready to strike if your opponent opens a line of attack or backs up, and feint before immobilizing with the trap. Safety and success depend on this.

Volume 1 has an entire chapter devoted to trapping, but even then, we just skimmed the surface of a rather complicated and often misunderstood subject. Because of that, we will focus on several specific points in this section: a simple energy drill, some basic trapping exercises and some *pak sao* (slapping-hand) progressions.

The energy drill will address how an opponent can only move so many ways when you make contact with him. He will give four kinds of energy, and the drills will show how to respond to them. Your responses should be practiced so you can do them instantly, without thought. After you have worked on all four responses, the trainer should do any of the energies while you respond with the correct reaction. You should also practice energy drills with your eyes closed because you are trying to learn to respond to an opponent's movement through sensitivity (touch) rather than sight.

For basic trapping exercises, the student and instructor should use the following list as a progressive guide during training. As mentioned in other parts of this book, begin by doing the points on the list from a stationary position. From there, add movement wherein the trainer and/or student moves forward or back. The student and trainer probably won't get through the entire list in one or several sessions. They should take their time. The list is as follows:

- The student practices trapping before, during and after the trainer hits.
- The student practices trapping with a pak sao and a backfist during the trainer's recovery. In other words, the trainer punches at the student. The student parries or uses distance. As the trainer's punch retracts, the student traps with a pak sao and hits with a backfist.
- From a high reference point, the student practices all the traps listed in Volume 1, such as the pak sao, *lop sao, huen sao, jao sao* and *jut sao*. He responds to how the trainer defends against the trap.
- The student does all the traps listed in Volume 1, but this time the student does them from a low reference point.
- The student practices going from a low straight lead punch to a high straight lead punch to a trap, or the reverse.
- The student practices a kick-to-hit-to-trap combination.

- The student uses an ABD to draw a hand attack from the trainer and then trap it.
- The student practices going from an ABC or PIA to a trap.
- From the high reference point, the student traps and hits when he feels the trainer move back.

In regards to the pak sao progression, begin your training by starting at a reference point, like the high or low outside reference point. Then work on various methods to bridge the gap and attain a point of contact to trap. After you have practiced these first two steps with a trainer, work on bridging the gap by feinting.

Simple Energy-Drill Response No. 1

A: Tim Tackett (right) faces his trainer. They hold their lead hands at a high outside reference point, giving each other a point of contact.

B: The trainer gives forward energy by pushing forward with his lead hand on the reference point.

Continued →

C: Tackett responds with a *lop sao* (grabbing hand) and straight rear punch. Learn more about the lop sao on pages 133-134 of Volume 1.

Simple Energy-Drill Response No. 2

A: The trainer and Tackett maintain a point of contact at the high outside reference point.

B: The trainer moves Tackett's lead arm to the left.

C: Tackett goes with the flow by relaxing his elbow and doing a lop sao to the inside of the trainer's arm.

D: Tackett hits with a backfist.

Simple Energy-Drill Response No. 3

A: Tackett and his trainer keep their lead hands in contact at a high outside reference point.

B: The trainer raises Tackett's arm by pushing up.

C, D, E: Tackett counters with a pak sao and hit. Note: If this were another scenario, Tackett could have parried to the outside and hit low with a straight lead punch. Learn more about the pak sao on pages 127-133 of Volume 1.

Simple Energy-Drill Response No. 4

A: Tackett and his trainer keep their hands in contact at a high outside reference point.

B: When the trainer attempts to hit low, Tackett responds with a downward parry and hit.

C: He ends with a hit.

Basic Trapping Exercise No.1

A: Tackett and his trainer stand at a high outside reference point.

B: When Tackett feel his trainer step back, he push-steps forward.

C: When he push-steps forward, he does a pak sao with a hit.

Basic Trapping Exercise No. 2

A: Tackett and his trainer face each other from the fighting measure.

B: Tackett push-steps forward to throw a backfist and bridge the gap. He doesn't want to land the hit so much as to gain an attachment. Note how the attachment occurs at the high outside reference point.

C: Tackett is then able to do a pak sao with a hit. Note: The trainer could also use this as an opportunity to see if Tackett is telegraphing. If he feels the trap, the trainer would just step back out of range.

Basic Trapping Exercise No. 3

A: Tackett and his trainer are at a long enough range that they can only make contact with the backs of their hands. Note: To work on a powerful push forward, start from a long range with your wrists touching your trainer's. Then thrust forward with a pak sao and hit.

B: As Tackett push-steps forward, he does a pak sao to the trainer's arm.

C: Having bridged the gap, Tackett has trapped the trainer's arm and scored with a straight lead punch. Note: When practicing trapping from such long distance, you have to thrust forward with great acceleration, so you must be very careful to control your punch so you do not injure your partner.

Basic Trapping Exercise No. 4

A: For reaction training, in this example, Tackett and his trainer have their hands at the high reference point with no pressure at all. The trainer then gives a slight pressure with his arm, and Tackett immediately traps and hits. Tackett uses a pak sao or lop sao.

Basic Trapping Exercise No. 5

A: Tackett and his trainer stand at the fighting measure.

B: The trainer executes a straight lead punch, and Tackett parries and keeps contact with the trainer's arm.

C: As the trainer retracts the attacking hand, Tackett attacks on recovery.

Basic Trapping Exercise No. 6

A: Tackett and his trainer stand at the fighting measure.

B: The trainer attacks with a straight lead punch.

C: Tackett sticks to the punching arm on the trainer's recovery. He follows it back and traps the rear hand by grabbing it, as if in a jut sao. Now Tackett has effectively trapped both of the trainer's arms and can do an actual jut sao and hit. Learn more about the jut sao on pages 137-140 of Volume 1.

Pak Sao Progression No. 1

A: Tackett and his trainer stand at the fighting measure. Tackett needs to bridge the gap to pak sao.

B: To bridge the gap, Tackett does an attack on delivery. This also gives him a high outside reference point to do a pak sao.

C: Tackett completes the pak sao.

Pak Sao Progression No. 2

A: Tackett and his trainer are at the fighting measure. Tackett needs to bridge the gap and make a point of contact to trap.

B: Tackett attacks on preparation (or intention), before the trainer can hit. He does a pak sao.

Pak Sao Progression No. 3

A

B

A: Tackett and his trainer stand at the fighting measure. As in the other drills, Tackett must make a point of contact and bridge the gap to trap.

B: The trainer executes a straight lead punch, which Tackett parries. This establishes a point of contact, but Tackett doesn't execute a pak sao yet.

C

C: As the trainer retracts his punch, Tackett attacks on recovery. He moves in to execute a pak sao.

D: Tackett traps the trainer with a pak sao. This is different from Progression No. 1 because Tackett is trapping while the attacker is retracting his punch. With practice, Tackett will be able to stick to the retracting arm with his palm.

Defense Against HIAs

In addition to attacking with traps, you need to learn to defend against someone who is trying to trap you. This is known as second-stage trapping. The trap itself is called first-stage trapping. A whole book could be devoted to this subject, but the main techniques the Wednesday Night Group does are shown in this section. (Some teachers go so far as to teach third-stage trapping—you trap, your partner defends, you counterattack. If you want to try this, feel free to come up with some third-stage trapping on your own. Think hit!)

Pak Sao Defense No. 1

A: Tim Tackett and his trainer begin with their lead hands on the high outside reference point.

B, C: The trainer attempts to pak sao.

D, E: However, Tackett angles to the left with a pak sao and has a straight line in which to punch with his right hand.

Pak Sao Defense No. 2

A: Tackett and his trainer stand with their hands at the high outside reference point.

B: The trainer attempts a pak sao to Tackett's lead arm.

C: However, Tackett parries the hit and stop-kicks with a hook kick to the groin.

Lop Sao Defense

A: Tackett and his trainer continue their trapping defense training. They still stand with their lead hands at a high outside reference point.

B: The trainer executes a lop sao.

C: Tackett outside-parries the punch.

D: Tackett then does a lop sao to the punching arm.

E: Tackett then releases his grip and grabs the wrist of the hand that the trainer used to lop sao. Then, by pressing down with his forearm, Tackett traps both of the trainer's arms.

F: Tackett punches with his rear arm. This whole sequence may seem complicated and difficult, but it is much easier than it appears.

Jao Sao Defense

A: Tackett and his trainer stand with their lead hands at the high outside reference point.

B, C: When the trainer attempts to pak sao, Tackett counters with a jao sao.

D: Tackett then executes a high straight lead punch, although he could also have executed a low straight lead punch.

Arm-Raise Counter No. 1

A: Tackett and his trainer stand with their lead arms at the high outside reference point.

B, C: When the trainer tries a pak sao, Tackett raises his arm to counter with a lop sao to the trainer's front arm.

Arm-Raise Counter No. 2

A: Tackett and his trainer stand with their lead hands at the high outside reference point.

B: The trainer attempts a pak sao, but Tackett counters with a lop sao.

C: Tackett shoots a finger jab between the trainer's arms.

There are a lot of drills and techniques in this chapter. Some of them are fairly easy to understand and perform, while others are much more difficult. If you find that some are more difficult to do than others, try working on some easier ones or even an easier component of a more difficult one. For example, make sure that you've practiced the front kick and the lead hook kick enough before you try to do a PIA attack with a low-feinting front kick followed by a high hook kick to the head.

Realize also that not all the ways of attack will work against all types of opponents. Let's go through them:

- The single direct attack will work if you are faster than your opponent, have little or no preparation, or catch him while he is moving in a vulnerable position whereby he cannot stop-hit or stop-kick you. The single angular attack will give you a better chance to score a hit because it is usually harder to stop-hit an attack off the centerline; most people practice stop-hits against direct attacks.

- Attacks by combination will usually work best as follow-ups after a stop-hit or stop-kick against an attacking opponent or after you score with a single attack. The straight blasts are examples of combination attacks. In your training, you should practice breaking the rhythm of your opponent's attempted combination attacks. Remember that you are not always able to stop-hit an opponent and may have to parry his initial attack. If that happens, you should try to hit him either before his second attack can land or on the one-and-a-half beat. The opposite is true if you attack and are blocked. In that case, you may want to retreat or to follow up your attack by using broken rhythm.
- Progressive indirect attacks are dangerous unless you are sure your opponent will block or use distance against your attack. Any time you feint, you are leaving an opening that an opponent can use to stop-hit you.
- Attacking by drawing can be a safe way to draw an attack so you can stop-hit an opponent. To be successful using ABD, you need to be sure to stay at the fighting measure to give yourself time to respond to your opponent's attack. You will also need to learn to see an adversary's preparation and take advantage of an opening. This is one of the main reasons that you should take a lot of time working with the hammer principle.
- Hand-immobilization attacks (trapping) are very useful to tie up one or more of your opponent's limbs. The Wednesday Night Group spends most of our trapping practice on trapping before, during or after an opponent attacks. Although it is important to work on energy drills and to practice trapping from the various reference points, it is important to practice trapping realistically against an "alive" opponent. When I use the term "alive," I refer to an opponent who is actively trying to counter what you are attempting to do.

When working on any of the five ways of attack, the sooner you make your practice alive, the better. Remember that in combat your opponent will be trying to counter everything you are trying to do to him. It's better to discover what works or does not work in a safe, controlled environment than in the street with no trainer or referee. One of the best ways to do that is to spar with the various tools. Some of the drills we use to develop sparring skills are discussed in the next chapter.

Chapter 7
SPARRING

As we discussed in Chapter 4, there are primary fighting tools that make up your basic fighting techniques. With each basic technique, like the straight lead punch, you should do the following:

- Work on perfecting it in the drills shown in other chapters.
- Practice it with all appropriate footwork.
- Practice attacking with it.
- Practice defending against it.

Once you feel comfortable with the above, you can start sparring with the basic technique. There are two main ways to work on sparring: restricted and open sparring. Restricted sparring is when you are limiting the hand and kicking tool you can use. This is how sparring practice actually begins—slow and without full punch or kicking speed or power. Open sparring is when there is no limit to using tools.

However, even then, you must remember to do certain things while open sparring. Too many times students are introduced to open sparring before they are ready for it, and as a result, they are injured, get discouraged or drop out. That's why it's important for you and your partner to practice safe sparring—like catching and rolling—as described in Chapter 5. In this regard, you also need to make sure you can trust your partner and that he has control, and vice versa. And finally, when sparring, try to avoid ego. There's nothing to prove, so there's no reason to get injured. You're both here to relax, learn and improve. Start with restricted sparring; work on a specific tool to attack and defend against, or both. Then work up to open sparring.

Training Tips

Make sure you have the proper equipment because safety is always the first concern in sparring. Too many students drop out because trainers or instructors don't know how to introduce their students safely to sparring.

For sparring, you'll need the following items:

- **Boxing gloves.** You'll want 14- or 16-ounce ones. Don't start with MMA-style gloves, which do not offer enough protection.
- **Mouthpiece.** People often have a tendency to spar with their mouths open, and that is why a mouthpiece is essential to protect your teeth from strikes. It also gives you

something to bite down on so your jaw remains closed; this will help protect against a broken jaw.

- **Headgear.** If you are going to do any hard sparring with powerful punches to the head, headgear is a good idea; it will offer some protection.
- **Shin guards.** JKD practitioners tend to do a lot of shin/knee kicking when sparring, so good shin guards are essential.

When beginning your sparring practice, start slow with restricted sparring. There's no rush. Use only one tool at a time and recover from each execution. This not only limits the tools at the trainer's disposal, it also helps the student feel more in control because he has an idea of how he will be attacked. The trainer shouldn't attack at full speed or power so the student can build up his skills. Once the student is able to defend and attack against specific tools, it's time to add more and more into the mix.

A good training progression to go by is as follows:

- The trainer hits with a straight lead punch while the student defends against it. In this example, the straight lead punch is used, but any tool can be used.
- The trainer and student try to attack with the tool they are defending against. For example, the trainer attacks with a straight lead punch while the student stop-hits with a straight lead punch.
- Once the student can attack and defend against the straight lead punch, he and the trainer will add another lead-hand tool, like the high hook. They will keep adding tools until all lead-hand tools are included.
- The student and trainer practice the scenarios already described in matched and unmatched leads.
- They add in all low-front-hand techniques.
- Once the student is proficient with using the front hand, the trainer and student will spar with front-hand attacks. They will also practice by having the trainer attack with the front hand while the student defends with the front hand, and vice versa.
- The trainer and student start adding front-leg tools with the front-hand tools. Like the first step in the progression, the trainer attacks with a kicking tool while the student defends against it.
- Then the student and trainer work on sparring with front-hand and front-leg tools only. They should start with a single hand attack against a single leg attack or vice versa. They should add other tools only one at a time.

It is only after all these steps that the trainer and student should add the rear hand. Bruce Lee believed that in combat you should use the front hand and foot the majority of the time. This is because the front hand and foot are closer to the target and make interception more efficient. It's also why one of the main principles in JKD is to keep the strong hand and foot forward.

Another shorthand way to consider the above progression is with this one:

- Spar with hands only.
- Spar with feet only.
- Spar with front hand against rear hand only.
- Spar with all hands against all feet.
- Add grappling defense.
- Add your own ideas.
- All-out open sparring with all tools.
- Work all from both matched and unmatched stances.

These are just some of the ways we work on sparring with various tools. Make sure to start slow and only add power a little at a time. The idea is to make the student feel confident and safe when sparring. Bruce Lee found at the Chinatown school that when students started heavy sparring, the dropout rate soared. Some of our students have jobs in which they deal with the public and don't want to go to work with a black eye or split lip. Some students may want to enter the ring and do a lot of hard sparring and not worry about being injured. If a teacher wants to do a lot of hard full-contact sparring, he may end up with a small group of hard-core fighters. That may be what he wants. Others may want a large group of students and not have most of them drop out once the sparring starts. How much sparring you do and how hard you do it is entirely up to each individual teacher and group. One way to introduce sparring is with the drills in this chapter. There are a lot of them, so feel free to pick and choose the ones you feel will work best for you. I've put these drills in here as a springboard for the reader to create his own.

Basic Sparring Drills

There are many different kinds of basic sparring drills. At their simplest, they are two-person glove drills wherein the trainer and student spar with equipment. In the Wednesday Night Group, we often practice stop-hits and stop-kicks. Since defending against attack with one of these is a basic principle of JKD defense, it's important to spend a lot of time with them. To do them, the trainer initiates a single hand or foot attack, and the student counters with a stop-hit or stop-kick. The trainer might also eventually mix high and low and lead- and rear-hand strikes.

In the Wednesday Night Group, the drills progress as follows:

- The trainer initiates any kick. The student stop-hits or uses distance, then returns a kick.
- The trainer uses any hand tool while the student uses stop-hits or other evasions.
- The trainer uses all kicking tools while the student can only use stop-hits and evasions.
- The trainer uses any ABC attack while the student can only use distance on the first attack, followed by a stop-hit or stop-kick on the second attack.

- The trainer mixes tools, footwork, stances and line so the student can't anticipate which punch is coming and how it will be executed. He must learn to react properly or be hit.

The second kind of sparring drills to be discussed are sparring with trapping practice. In these drills, the trainer attacks the student with either a straight lead punch or jab. The student then traps and attacks on delivery or on recovery. The student can also do a leg obstruction followed by a trap.

The third kind of sparring drills to be discussed are exchange drills. In these kinds of drills, the trainer attacks and the student must return the same attack. For example, the trainer might kick with a lead side kick. The student will use distance to defend, then return the same kick. The trainer will then retreat and throw the same kick, a hand attack or something different. Another example is that the trainer attacks with an SDA or SAA, then follows with an ABC with steady or broken rhythm. Come up with as many combinations as possible, and keep coming back to them if the open sparring starts to get out of control.

There are also variations of catch drills. Simply put, to vary a catch drill, do the following:

- Catch a punch, then return it or another hand tool.
- Catch the punch and trap.
- Parry the punch.

Two-Person Sparring: Jab Defense to Leg Obstruction

A: Jeremy Lynch (right) and Dennis Blue face off in fighting stances with gloves.

B: Lynch jabs at Blue, and Blue catches the punch with the palm of his glove while sliding up.

C, D: He slides up to do a leg obstruction. Note: In practicing the leg obstruction, the trainer should wear a shin guard to protect himself from injury.

E: Blue then hits with a straight lead punch, which Lynch catches with his rear glove.

F: Blue then strikes with a straight rear punch while Lynch shoulder-rolls to avoid being hit.

Leg Obstruction Used as a Stop-Kick

A, B: This time when Lynch attempts to jab, Blue intercepts with a leg obstruction.

C, D: Blue then attacks Lynch with a straight lead punch-and-hook combination. Lynch catches the straight lead punch and covers against the hook.

Two-Person Sparring: Catch and Return With Slip

A

A: Lynch and Blue stand at the fighting measure.

B

B: Lynch jabs, and Blue catches it.

C

C: He returns Lynch's jab.

D

D: After catching Blue's jab, Lynch returns another jab, but this time, Blue slips the punch and strikes with a low straight lead punch.

Two-Person Sparring: Bob and Weave to Knee Strike

A: Lynch and Blue stand at the fighting measure.

B: Blue push-steps forward to deliver a front hook punch, but Lynch covers.

C: Lynch moves to return a hook.

D, E: Blue bobs and weaves under it.

F: He then hits Lynch with a knee strike to the lead thigh.

Two-Person Sparring: Complicated Series

A: Lynch and Blue face off at the fighting measure.

B: Lynch hits Blue with a 1 – 2 combination. Blue avoids the first hit with a catch.

C: He avoids the second of Lynch's hits with a shoulder roll.

D: Blue returns a straight rear punch (the 2 – 3 combination). Lynch shoulder-rolls away.

E, F: Blue finishes the combination with a front hook, but Lynch bobs and weaves under it.

G: Lynch returns a straight rear punch, but Blue shoulder-rolls.

H: Blue returns the straight rear punch, but Lynch slips inside.

I: Lynch weaves under it.

J: From this position, Lynch is able to hit Blue by leaning back to deliver a straight lead.

The Wall-Survival Drill

Sometimes when you spar or are in combat, you get your bell rung, meaning your opponent hits you so hard that you become dazed. This makes you vulnerable and gives your opponent more opportunities to continue hitting you. That's why in training you need to work on surviving until you get all your mental faculties back so you are better able to defend yourself. You'll need to work on surviving a few punches until you are able to clinch and prevent your opponent from continuing his attack. This is the purpose of the wall-survival drill. (This drill is an old boxing routine that I first learned from Bert

Poe, a former combat veteran, police officer, boxer, tracker and judo instructor. He passed away in 1992 but remains an important part of our group. Hardly a class goes by without our using one of his training methods.)

The wall drill is also a great drill for anyone wishing to enter any form of full-contact fighting. I know that MMA fighter and trainer Erik Paulson uses it in his training.

The wall-survival drill has two main purposes. The first is to learn to take a punch and be able to survive an onslaught of blows without panicking. The second is to learn to clinch at different beats.

To do the wall-survival drill, the student stands against something that he can lean on. It may be a wall, a heavy bag or the ropes in a boxing ring. Whatever you lean on, you want to be in a position in which you can't move back. The trainer will then hit to the student's body and head.

At the start of the drill, the student's arms should be in a pillar defense with both gloves protecting the sides of his head and his elbows tucked in to protect his midsection as much as possible. The trainer, at a cue from the student, will start punching with a series of close-range punches like hooks, uppercuts and shovel hooks to the student's head and body. No punches below the belt; knee and elbow strikes aren't allowed either. The trainer and the student should both have 16-ounce boxing gloves on. The student should also be wearing a mouthpiece.

The important things to keep in mind are:

- The student must have a strong defense and roll or cover. He could also drop his body to cover his midsection with his elbows and forearms.
- The student may choose to take some blows to his midsection to toughen it up.
- The student is in complete control of how hard and fast the trainer punches. He does this by calling out things like "faster," "slower," "harder" or "softer."
- The student must have complete confidence in the trainer and not feel that he will be injured.

No more than three punches should be thrown at the student before he clinches unless you are doing timed rounds where he is taking a series of punches for a set period of time.

There are two basic ways to do these drills. The first is to do them in rounds at a set time—anything from 30 seconds to 3 or more minutes. The second way is to let the trainer get in a set number of punches before the student clinches. A clinch is one of the best ways to survive the onslaught of an attacker who is striking repeatedly. In the Wednesday Night Group, we practice clinching in this drill on the half-beat. What is a beat? Here's what I mean: If a trainer throws three punches, that is three beats of time. If the student clinches after the third punch and before the fourth is launched, he is clinching on the three-and-a-half beat. Between the third and second punches is the two-and-a-half beat. And after the first punch but before the second punch is the one-and-a-half beat. So what beat is before the first punch has a chance to land? It's the half-beat. In combat, JKD practitioners want to clinch on the fewest number of beats possible to avoid injury, so while we work on all beats, we prefer to clinch on the half.

For all wall-survival drills, the trainer should remember to start slow and then pick up the pace. He should mix combination punches as well as break in with a series of blows, then step back, then come in again. The trainer should also step in at different angles—diagonal-left and -right as well as straight—and change rhythm, distance and speed and fake or feint his way in.

Timed-Rounds Training

A: Jeremy Lynch leans against a wall. Dennis Blue waits for a cue to start.

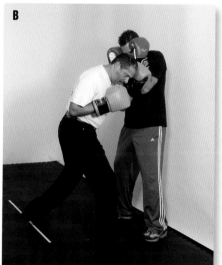

B: After the cue, Blue punches at Lynch's head and midsection. Lynch keeps his hands up and elbows tucked in for defense.

C: Blue hits Lynch with a shovel hook.

D: He then strikes with a rear hook to Lynch's head. Notice how Lynch is twisting to cover and parry the punches.

E: Blue then hits with a front hook.

F: Finally, Blue hits with a rear uppercut.

Clinching on Half-Beats

A: Blue is close to Lynch, who has covered up.

B: Blue hits Lynch with a rear uppercut.

C: Blue then hits Lynch with a lead upper-cut, which Lynch catches on his glove.

D: Blue then hits Lynch with a rear hook to the head.

E: Before Blue can punch a fourth time, Lynch clinches on the three-and-a-half beat. He wraps his arms around Blue to prevent his strikes.

Clinching on Half-Beats (Other Scenarios)

  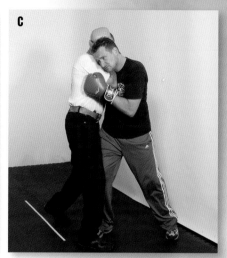

A, B, C: This time Blue gets in only two hits before Lynch clinches on the two-and-a-half beat.

D, E, F: Lynch clinches on the one-and-a-half beat.

G, H, I: This time Lynch clinches on the half-beat, while Blue is in the process of throwing the first punch.

The "Psycho" Drill

If you want to see how a student will react under pressure, the "psycho" drill is a great method. The drill works like this:

Three students with boxing gloves and mouthpieces stand in a line about two feet apart from each other and facing the trainer, who has his back to them. The reason there are at least three students is that they will not be able to figure out which one the trainer will attack and there will be an element of surprise. Without warning, the trainer spins and starts attacking one of the students with fast and heavy—but not very hard—punches. The trainer will find that many students, even some with experience in sparring, will still get surprised when the trainer turns and they will cower in response; it is a more natural response than clinching or intercepting. Practice will eventually train the student not to do this but to intercept, cover or clinch. When doing the drill, the trainer must turn and hit at the targeted student very fast with heavy off-angle punches that do not penetrate or harm the student attacked. But unless the student feels threatened, the drill will not work. To add to the surprise and shock, the trainer can scream as he turns. This drill is difficult to do and takes a lot of practice as both the trainer and the student can be injured unless they both have a lot of control. This drill should be considered an advanced one and should only be used after the student has sparred a lot.

Environmental Sparring

Once you have practiced against one opponent, feel comfortable sparring, and trust your fellow students or trainers, you can add environmental-sparring drills to your training. Make sure you start slow because it's easy for some of these drills to get out of control, and injuries are possible. Both trainer and student should try to stay relaxed and as calm as possible.

The following is a list of scenarios practiced by the Wednesday Night Group:

- One student spars against two opponents.
- Two students spar against three opponents.
- Two students spar against four opponents.
- The student and his fellow practitioners do the alley drill, wherein cones are placed on the ground to simulate an alley. Four trainers come down the alley toward two students. The four trainers attack the two students. The students' objective is to fight their way through the group and escape the alley.
- The student and trainer spar with the lights out.
- The student and trainer place different obstacles or objects in the room to either be avoided or used during their sparring session.
- The student spars while pretending that one arm is injured and he can't use it. The student can also pretend that his leg is injured and his mobility is limited.
- The student must escape after the trainer traps him against a wall or piece of furniture.

- The student practices defending from the ground, as if he were knocked down or lost his footing. He must work on safely and quickly getting back to his feet.
- The student and trainer work on escaping from all positions on the ground. They work on all kinds of foul tactics as well as traditional escapes.
- The student and trainer create their own situations.

Sparring should be an important part of any JKD training for many reasons. First, it lets you know what your weaknesses are in both your attack and defense strategies. If you can't make it work in sparring, you should not try it in a street confrontation. Sparring allows you to experiment with different attacks and defenses against various opponents. It's always better to learn what works in a class environment than on the street. Second, restricted sparring helps you hone a particular attack or defensive maneuver in a controlled environment. For example, if you only slip against your sparring partner's straight punches, you will become more efficient using them in unrestricted sparring. Third, it teaches you how to roll with the punches or clinch to survive until you are able to counterattack. Even though jeet kune do's preferred defense is an interception, sometimes you may be too close to intercept or be surprised, and that's when you'll have to roll with a punch or clinch.

But remember to start slow and easy. Take time adding power to your strikes. Sparring is the time to experiment and see what works. Don't be afraid to try new things. And above all, be safe!

Chapter 8
MISCELLANEOUS TRAINING METHODS

The following drills are those that don't quite fit into any of the other chapters. While there are awareness drills throughout this book, this chapter will go into a little more detail on them. This chapter also includes the basic hammer-principle drill. Even though this drill is included in Volume 1, I feel it is so important to JKD training that it is included again here. Some basic balance drills are also included because they are an important attribute to using your attack and defense tools. I hope that they will be of value to you and that you can create your own. The Wednesday Night Group has also borrowed some of the balance drills we do from other arts like *savate* and *taekwondo*. Lastly, I've included two distance drills in this chapter as well as a quick explanation of shadowboxing and a short description of emotional-content training.

Awareness Drills

Awareness drills are a big part of JKD training because they teach students to react properly to a stimulus. In fact, we've already talked about lots of different kinds of awareness drills. For example, in Chapter 3, you may have noticed how drills indicated that the trainer uses a visual cue, like a raised finger. By using a visual cue, the student will then know to kick or punch. Some other visual cues that have occurred routinely in the book for focus-glove training are the trainer raising his foot, lowering his body, taking a step forward, etc.

Trainers can also use focus gloves in awareness drills to feed certain lines to students. This means that the trainer makes the student aware of the proper stimulus, such as the position of the glove, so the student can react with the proper combat tool. Here are some cues the trainer can feed to the student:

- single hand attacks
- single kicks
- hand-tool combinations
- kicking-tool combinations
- hand-to-foot-tool combinations
- foot-to-hand-tool combinations
- knee and elbow strikes

For awareness training with the heavy bag, hang one from the ceiling at your house or gym. This drill works on your awareness while you practice kicking and punching the bag. To do the drill: The trainer stands behind the bag. He will have his shoulder against the bag to support it when the student either kicks or punches it. The student punches or kicks the bag based on cues from the trainer. If he wants the student to kick, the trainer will raise his leg. If he wants the student to punch, he will raise his hand. The student will then react to the stimulus with the proper response. This falls in line with the basic principles of jeet kune do, which say to react to any situation at a moment's notice with the proper response.

Here are two other awareness drills:

- **Flashlight-on-the-Wall Drill:** With the lights dim or out, the trainer shines a flashlight on a wall. He moves the flashlight around the wall. When he stops the flashlight, that is the cue for the student to strike in the direction of the light. This drill can be done with a group of students facing a wall. They will then hit or kick the air when the cue is given.

- **Click-the-Sticks Drill:** In this drill, the trainer stands in front of the student, or students; the student faces him. He clicks two sticks together as a cue for a certain reaction. For example, if he clicks the sticks once, the student could do a specific punch. If he clicks them twice, he could do a specific kick. You can do this type of drill with footwork too. The student could move forward on one click or back on two. The trainer could click the sticks two times very fast to have the students move forward or backward quickly, or once to just move forward or backward one time.

There are many group drills that will work with many of the kicking and hand-tool techniques discussed in this book. Below are just a few examples of the many that you can create.

- **Three-Person Equipment Awareness Drill:** Have the student stand with three trainers around him at 12, 3 and 9 o'clock. The trainers hold shields or focus gloves. The main trainer stands directly behind the student. He silently points to each of the three other trainers in turn. At his signal, the indicated trainer feeds the student an attack by stepping forward slightly. For example, a trainer with a focus glove feeds a hook-kick cue while another feeds a side-kick cue with a shield. The stimulus comes from the trainer's cue. The student must then respond with the correct hit or kick. When a person is attacked, the attacker will usually leave an opening. Drills like these will help your counterattack awareness.

- **Two-Group Awareness Drills:** This first drill involves the student standing in a circle of five or six trainers. Each trainer is given a number. The main trainer calls a number. The trainer whose number is called then attacks the student, who then defends. In the second drill, the student stands in the center of a circle surrounded by five or six other students. Each student is given a number. When the trainer calls a number, that student attacks the student in the center. As the class progresses, the trainer may call two or three numbers to attack the student in the center at the same time. Now the student in the center must respond to a multiple-attack scenario. In later scenarios, the center student can close his eyes while the surrounding students weave around him to different positions. This way the center student will not know from which direction he will be attacked; he also won't know where the students with numbers will be located when they are called to attack him.

The picture sequences show examples of stimulus-response drills. The student and trainer should practice each drill. When the student is able to react to each stimulus correctly, the trainer should begin mixing up his reactions. The trainer wants to respond to the student's initial attack differently each time so that the student's reaction is based on what is there rather than what the student thinks will be there. The student's instant reaction will then be "alive," like in a real combat situation. There are many ways to mix up the techniques, footwork and responses in stimulus-response drills. You should try to come up with as many ways as you can to vary your training methods.

Stimulus-Response Drill No. 1

A: Dennis Blue and Tim Tackett Jr. square off at the fighting measure.

B: Tackett Jr. takes a slight step forward and throws a backfist. Blue, the trainer, blocks with a lead-hand upper block, which leaves the lower part of his body exposed.

C, D: Tackett Jr., seeing the opening, steps forward to cover the distance and hits Blue with a low straight rear punch.

Stimulus-Response Drill No. 2

A, B, C: This time when Tackett Jr. tries to hit Blue with a straight lead punch, Blue uses distance to defend.

D, E: Tackett Jr. then kicks to bridge the gap.

Stimulus-Response Drill No. 3

A, B, C: This time when Tackett Jr. punches, Blue parries and then changes levels to try for a single-leg takedown.

D: Tackett Jr. defends against the attack by angling away from it.

E, F: He hits with an upward finger strike to Blue's eyes.

High/Low Stimulus-Response Drill

A, B, C: Blue executes a straight lead punch with his rear hand high. Meanwhile, Tackett parries the hit and strikes low.

D, E, F: This time, Blue drops his hand low as he hits, but Tackett parries and hits high to the open line. Note: After practicing this drill for a while, Blue will mix keeping his rear hand high or low, and Tackett will have to learn awareness to relate.

Hammer Principle

The hammer principle is one of the most valuable techniques in jeet kune do and one of the least known and understood. Because the principle is so difficult to do correctly, many students either give up or dismiss the technique entirely. Once you have become relatively proficient with the hammer principle, however, you will quickly realize just how deceptive it is.

I can't emphasize enough how important this drill is. This drill will help the student get rid of his preparation. If the trainer keeps parrying the student's finger jab, he is reading the student's preparation. If the trainer tells him what he sees and the student starts hitting with greater success, the student will be able to attack with more and more efficiency. The person who is acting as the trainer also benefits from this exercise because he needs to look out for the student's preparation to attack. If he can see it coming, he can stop-hit or stop-kick it. The more the trainer gets rid of the student's preparation, the harder the student's attack is to see. If they keep working on it enough, the trainer will learn to react to the subtlest cues from the student. When first learning this drill, start in stationary stances. As trainer and student improve, they should do the drill while moving. Learn more about the hammer principle on pages 153-156 of Volume 1.

Why the Hammer Drill Is Important

A: Jeremy Lynch and Tim Tackett face each other in fighting stances.

B: Tackett attempts to execute a finger jab.

C: Lynch notices Tackett's preparation and parries the strike.

D: They both recover to their fighting stances. Note: Working on the hammer principle will eventually help Tackett get rid of his preparation.

E: Tackett uses the hammer principle this time; he drops his fist as if pounding a nail to mask his step forward.

F: Tackett is able to score his hit now.

Balance Drills

You've already learned many balance drills in this book, but here are a few more:

- **Savate Warm-up Drill:** This drill is a common one in savate training that the Wednesday Night Group uses. To do the drill, the trainer stands with his arms straight out. The student then holds his leg straight out and weaves it around the trainer's arms in a figure-eight pattern.
- **Concentration Drill:** This is a great balance drill from taekwondo. The student and trainer touch fingertips. Then the student balances on one leg to chamber and kick.
- **Basic Balance Drill:** This is also a great balance drill from taekwondo. The student stands on one leg while holding the other in front of him. He then moves it in different directions while attempting to keep his balance. The student keeps his arms in a ready position.

Savate Warm-Up Drill: Front Kick

A, B, C, D, E: Vince Raimondi stands with his arms extended so Patrick Cunningham can practice his balance. He does a figure eight around Raimondi's arms from a front-kick position.

Savate Warm-Up Drill: Side Kick

A, B, C, D, E, F: Raimondi stands with his arms extended so Cunningham can practice his balance. He does a figure eight around Raimondi's arms from a side-kick position.

Concentration Drill

A, B, C: Raimondi and Cunningham touch fingers. Cunningham chambers and executes a side kick.

D, E, F: Cunningham shifts his feet and chambers to execute a front kick.

Defensive Distance Drills

When writing the book, I was originally unable to decide if these drills should go into Chapter 5 or Chapter 6 on defense and attacks, as they are a way to practice both. So I put them here.

These drills are designed to help the student control the distance between him and his opponent. They will also help the student learn to read the opponent's attack so he can intercept it.

The three drills are as follows:

- **Reading-the-Kick Drill:** The student starts from beyond the fighting measure, facing the trainer. The trainer throws a side kick or a front kick to the student's knee. However, that's not the important part of the drill. Before the trainer executes the kick, the student looks for preparation or intention, so he can then use distance to defend. As training progresses over time, the trainer will move closer and closer until he and the student are only a few inches apart. Note: Make sure to only move back enough to have the kick just miss you. This is one of Wednesday Night Group instructor Jim McCann's basic drills. In the Wednesday Night Group, we've learned that this drill helps students learn how to retreat and counterattack quickly and without leaving any room or time for the opponent to renew his attack.

- **Intercepting Distance Drill:** The trainer will throw either a hand or foot from beyond the fighting measure, while the student just watches to see preparation and intention. He does not react. Instead, he just observes and looks for when he could stop-hit. He thinks about how he will intercept the strike by using a stop-kick against a hand attack and a stop-hit against a kick. After a few lessons doing this, the trainer moves closer and closer until he's at the fighting measure. The student will then either stop-hit or stop-kick that trainer's attack.

- **Touch-the-Shirt Drill:** This is a drill that was done at the Chinatown school as well as Dan Inosanto's backyard class. The purpose of the drill is to teach the student to use just enough distance when retreating from a kick so he can counterattack efficiently. This close-as-possible distance gives the student two advantages: (a) The trainer won't have enough room to renew his offense with a second kick, and (b) the student will be close enough to counterattack before the trainer has a chance to follow up his first attack with a kick or hand attack. If the timing is right, the student can even deliver his counterattack before the trainer's kicking leg touches the ground. To do the drill, the student and trainer face each other at the fighting measure in fighting stances. The trainer has his back to the wall. He will throw a light side kick to the student's stomach; the trainer should kick at the same depth he would in a real attack. If the student doesn't retreat, he will be kicked. He needs to judge the distance needed so the kick barely misses him. The idea is that the trainer's kick should touch the student's T-shirt but not his body. The trainer will continue to kick and the student will retreat until the student reaches the opposite wall. Then the two practitioners switch roles. As the student and trainer get better at the drill, the kicks get harder.

Reading-the-Kick Drill

A, B, C: From beyond the fighting measure, Vince Raimondi kicks at Patrick Cunningham's leg. Cunningham uses distance to defend.

D, E, F: When Cunningham can successfully retreat from beyond the fighting measure, he and Raimondi move to a closer range.

G, H, I: When Cunningham can successfully retreat from that range, he and Raimondi move even closer to do the drill.

Shadow Boxing

One of the best ways to see how a single student or a group is progressing is to have them shadow-box for one or two rounds as part of their warm-up. Tell them to visualize an opponent and to move around as they kick and hit. The trainer will be able to see if the student is imaginative in his movement, has too much preparation, keeps his balance, etc.

Like with other progressions in this book, there are a lot of ways to add to, edit and approach shadow boxing. You can start simple by throwing one or two tools. You can eventually add movement and start mixing rhythms. Be creative!

Emotional-Content Training

Emotional content is nothing more than controlled anger. With anger, you can have a tendency to lose control. With emotional-content training, you can turn anger on and off like a light switch. In a famous scene in *Enter The Dragon*, Bruce Lee's character tells his young student to kick. Lee's character scolds the student for kicking with anger and tells the student to kick with emotional content instead. With emotional content, you can focus your whole being into hitting the target with tremendous force.

There are many ways to work on controlled anger in training. Some of the former military instructors the Wednesday Night Group has worked with have some great drills to achieve this, but this type of practice can be dangerous if it gets out of control. Any instructor, trainer or student must be careful with this type of training. If you and your partner can see that neither of you hit with passion but merely go through the motions, you can introduce some emotional-content training into your practice.

The most basic way to do this type of training is to have the trainer hold a kicking shield or focus glove. The student then hits or kicks it. If there is no real force in the blow, the trainer can tell the student to visualize something he hates on the focus glove or shield. It could be a person or an abstract idea, like prejudice. Whatever it is, it is something the trainer really doesn't need to know; it can remain secret. The student hits the focus glove with the idea that he's not hitting a glove but rather the thing he hates, and his punch or kick can destroy it.

If the student doesn't seem to "get it," the trainer can encourage him to close his eyes. The student should relax by slowly counting his breaths. The trainer will then tell the student to "go." When the trainer says that, the student is to open his eyes and hit the focus glove with all the power he can muster. Once the student seems relaxed, the trainer will describe a scenario in which someone the student loves is in danger and the only way to save that someone is for the student to destroy what is in front of him. This story should be as visual as possible. The student must see the person he loves in danger. The student must believe that he has the ability to save the loved one by acting with his whole being. The trainer will then yell "Go!," and the student hits the glove. Once he's hit it, the trainer will tell the student to relax. This will usually work to calm the student down, and the student will realize he has a tiger within him that he can control and release when he or his loved ones are in danger.

I must stress again that this method of training is difficult and should only be used with a student whom the trainer knows very well and who the trainer knows has good self-control.

Awareness drills are also important because they can help you see an opening when it occurs and then help you learn how to respond in the correct manner.

Some of the drills in this chapter are easy, and some are quite difficult. If you work on the balance exercises for a while, your balance will get better, and you will be more efficient in your attacks and defense. Shadow boxing will help you learn to visualize an opponent and then react to what he is doing with a move of your own. For example, you may imagine him attacking and you stop-kicking him. The distance drills can help you control your distance to your opponent so your counterattacks will be more efficient. The hammer-principle drill will help you get rid of your preparation and at the same time be able to see your opponent's. But as I've often mentioned, these drills are only a foundation, an inspiration. Don't be bound by any of them.

CONCLUSION

This book contains a lot of material, and I hope it gives you inspiration to last you for many years. I know my training has changed a lot, but the foundation I've built has allowed me to be creative. I also hope that you have fun with the drills in this book. Train with a partner. If you're the trainer, don't feel like you have to correct all the errors you see immediately. Work on helping the student eliminate them one by one. If you're the student, don't feel like you have to spend a lot of time on every technique or drill. Instead, try them for a while to see what works best for you. Then concentrate on those that benefit you the most for the time being. And use these drills as a springboard to create your own. I know I did.

I want to wish you the best of luck in your continued growth in *jeet kune do*. Just remember to try to get a little better each day. You will find that you will improve for a while before you hit a point where it seems you have stopped making progress on a particular technique. If this happens, try: taking a short break before coming back to it, varying your training and/or your routine, or working at it until you break through that wall. You must realize that everyone is different and what will work for one person may not work for another. Bruce Lee believed that it wasn't effective to try to make every student do the same thing in the same way.

Becoming a good martial artist requires a lot of work. It means adding variety, seeking out other practitioners and trying out your own ideas. Doing all this along with this book should make your training more interesting, and hence more enjoyable.

I would like to end this book with an explanation of just how the Wednesday Night Group trains. We try to take the few things we do most often and work on them about 80 percent of the time. We try to adhere to the principle of daily increase, which means we try to use the fewest tools to achieve the greatest results. We try to control our distance as much as possible and, when attacked, to intercept with enough power to end the attack. To do this efficiently, we try to limit our responses to a stimulus. Like Bruce Lee taught: If you are thrown something, simply catch it. To illustrate this, I usually tell the following story:

A man accidentally touches a hot stove. Without a thought, he immediately takes his hand off it and only suffers the slightest burn. One day, he is walking down the street and sees a sign that says "School of Taking Your Hand Off a Hot Stove." He goes into the school and is met by the master. The master asks him about his experience: How did the man take his hand off the hot stove? The man explains that he just took his hand off the stove and doesn't remember exactly how he did it. The master tells him what he did was very dangerous and that he must learn the correct method, which is to move your hand forward and up. The man signs up and practices the movement on a cold stove until he learns the proper method. Feeling that he still does not have enough techniques to really take his hand off a hot stove, he finds another school with a different method. In the end, he goes to seven different schools and practices seven different ways of taking his hand off a hot stove. One master teaches him to take it off in a clockwise motion, while another tells him to do it with a counterclockwise motion. After many years of practice, he finally feels that he has mastered the art of taking his hand off a hot stove. Even then, he still searches for a better way. Then one day, he accidentally puts his hand on a hot stove and is severely burned.

Keep Blasting,
Tim Tackett

GLOSSARY

Attack elements refer to the five stages that Bruce Lee taught his students to target during the development of an attack and its eventual defense. These stages are "attack on intention," "attack on preparation," "attack on delivery," "attack on completion," and "attack on recovery."

Attack on intention is the first stage addressed by attack elements. When someone wants to attack, the brain signals the body to perform the desired technique. Of course, this happens in less than a second, but it can still be enough time to give away an opponent's intention. That's why a *jeet kune do* stylist really wants to attack with nonintention, which means hitting without thought. (See "nonintention.")

Attack on preparation is the second stage addressed by the attack elements. When most people attack, they telegraph their intended attack in some way. For instance, before punching, an opponent may pull back his hand, tense his shoulder or make a face. A jeet kune do stylist uses this opportunity to intercept an attack before it's launched or, as Bruce Lee called it, to "stop him at the gate."

Attack on delivery is the third attack stage addressed by attack elements. If an opponent has started his punch, a jeet kune do practitioner hits back before the opponent's strike reaches its target. In essence, the JKD stylist intercepts the attack on the half-beat with a stop-hit. (See "beats.") This stops him from being able to make contact with the stylist or launch a second attack.

Attack on completion is the fourth stage addressed by the attack elements, and it refers to intercepting an attack when the opponent's arm is fully extended. This usually happens on the focal point or full beat. (See "focal point" and "beats.") In this stage, a jeet kune do practitioner may also take advantage of a fighter's tendency to overextend his punch.

Attack on recovery is the fifth stage of the attack elements and occurs when an adversary attempts to recover or return his attacking limb to its original starting point. In response, a JKD stylist launches a counter, which fencers call a "response hit." It also generally occurs on the one-and-a-half beat. (See "beats.")

Beats are measurements of time during an attack. For example, an opponent strikes with a straight lead punch. When the fist is midway between its original position and full extension, that is a half-beat of time. When the punch reaches full extension, that is one full beat of time. When the punch withdraws midway between full extension and its original place in the fighting stance, that is a one-and-a-half beat of time. If the opponent were to hit with a two-punch combination, like a jab and a rear straight punch, the rear punch would reach full extension on two beats of time. As the rear returns to its original position, that would be two-and-a-half beats of time. In *jeet kune do*, practitioners prefer to counter on half-beats whenever possible.

Body feel refers to when a martial artist has an implicit understanding of how his movements affect his balance and of where his body is at all times. While the concept sounds simple, it's actually something a lot of people fail to grasp because they don't have a good idea of where their body is in relationship to their surroundings. For example, if a person steps forward three inches with his front foot and six inches with his rear foot, then four inches with his front foot and two inches with his rear foot, his body feel is off because he is unaware that he is off-balance and not maintaining a uniform distance in his fighting stance. In *Tao of Jeet Kune Do*, Bruce Lee described body feel as "a harmonious interplay of body and spirit, both inseparable."

Bridging the gap is the space between two opponents when in the fighting measure. (See "fighting measure.") The gap is bridged when one of the opponents moves past the fighting measure into striking distance.

Brim-of-fire line is the distance at which either opponent can strike without moving forward because one has crossed the fighting measure. (See "fighting measure.")

Cadence is the specific rhythm for a succession of movements in a technique or combination.

Chi sao is a *wing chun* kung fu energy drill that allows a *jeet kune do* practitioner to feel and/or create openings in an opponent's defense. It is also called the "sticky hands" technique because it is an exercise whereby one partner feels the flow of his opponent's energy by sticking to his hands and movements. The technique is an especially useful training device for hand traps.

Classical technique is what Bruce Lee believed to be one of the problems with traditional martial arts. Because traditional students learn to attack in a predetermined pattern rather than in relationship to their opponent's movements, they are limited to a combination of predetermined moves from their style.

Clicks refer to the way Bruce Lee described a move's efficiency. If a technique is filmed, a *jeet kune do* practitioner can tell how efficient it is by the number of frames. Lee called each frame, or picture in the film, a click and said that a JKD practitioner should try to eliminate as many clicks as possible in his combat.

Commitment refers to how much power a *jeet kune do* practitioner puts into a technique.

"Half commitment" is like a boxing jab; it is a minor blow to set up a major blow. "Full commitment" is a major blow, which hits through the target but does not overextend. "Extension commitment" requires the JKD practitioner to throw everything he has at his target with no regard for recovery. This kind of attack, such as a stop-hit or stop-kick, he should only attempt when he is absolutely sure that he will hit the target with enough force to end the fight. Note: More powerful techniques take longer to recover from. If you miss with an overcommitted punch, you will probably be vulnerable to a counterattack.

Critical distance line is between the fighting measure and the brim-of-fire line. At this distance, either move back to intercept or move forward to build momentum and get the most power from an attack. By doing this, a *jeet kune do* practitioner gains the necessary power to penetrate two inches.

Deception masks a technique's true intent. For example, a *jeet kune do* stylist tricks his opponent into believing that he is attacking with a high hand strike but instead launches a low kick. Two of the five ways of attack—the attack by drawing and the progressive indirect attack—are based on deception and are discussed in Chapter 6.

Defensive movement patterns are predictable movements and footwork. In contrast, the *jeet kune do* martial artist wants to always be unpredictable.

Delayed hit is also known as a "broken-time attack." To do it, begin a strike, take a slight pause, and then renew the attack. A *jeet kune do* stylist uses delayed hits against an opponent who over-blocks. To take advantage of this, the stylist starts a punch, pauses when the opponent begins to block, and then renews the punch as soon as the block ends.

Distracting hand uses a *jeet kune do* practitioner's hands to focus his adversary's attention away from his intended attack. There are three hand-distracting methods: the "obstructing method," the "sound method" and the "combination method." Using the obstructing method, a jeet kune do stylist throws his front hand up to the level of his opponent's eyes while still in the fighting measure, mimicking a progressive indirect attack. This tricks his adversary into thinking that he will attack with his hands, but instead he's going to bridge the gap and attack with a low kick. The sound method, as the name implies, uses sound as a distraction, such as clapping your hands before an attack. The third method combines the first two. For example, a JKD practitioner might throw his front hand up and slap his thigh for effect before attacking.

Double time is a term Bruce Lee borrowed from fencing that refers to blocking an attack and following up with a *jeet kune do* practitioner's own move. For example, you might block a kick and then launch your own counterkick. However, be wary because double time is a passive defense. If an opponent feints a *jeet kune do* practitioner into a block, he has successfully deceived the practitioner. This means the opponent's hit will land before the JKD practitioner can muster a counter.

Drawing refers to when a *jeet kune do* stylist tricks an opponent into attacking by purposely leaving some part of his body unprotected and open. This provokes the opponent into thinking he can launch a successful attack, one that the JKD stylist already has a specific counter in mind for.

Fakes are done when a JKD practitioner wants his opponent to go in one direction while he moves in the other. In *jeet kune do*, there are three kinds of fakes: the eye fake, the body-position fake and the half-motion fake. To trick your opponent with an eye fake, look at one target, then attack another. For example, if the JKD practitioner plans on attacking low, he looks at his opponent's head. This makes the opponent think the practitioner is going to throw a high attack. A body-position fake means moving in one direction, then attacking the other. If a JKD stylist lowers his body as if he's going to strike at a low target, his opponent will think the stylist will hit low. The opponent will not expect a high attack. A half-motion fake refers to when a JKD stylist uses one of his limbs to distract his opponent from his true line of attack. Basically, it is an incomplete attack that deceives the opponent and opens a line.

Feints are not fakes. They are false attacks meant to confuse an opponent. When doing a continuous motion, like a kick or punch, the motion should seem like a real attack until the *jeet kune do* practitioner switches to his true line of attack.

Fencing terms are often interchangeable with martial arts terms in *jeet kune do* because of Lee's studies into Western fighting practices. Some common terms used by JKD practitioners include "on-guard," which refers to the fighting stance; "parry," which refers to a block; and "riposte," which refers to a hit that follows a block. (See also "double time.")

Fighting measure is the distance a *jeet kune do* practitioner wants to maintain between his opponent and himself. Because the opponent will need to step toward the practitioner to launch an attack, it is also the distance necessary to intercept an attack.

Focal point is the full beat between the opening and closing line of an attack.

Formless form means that *jeet kune do* is not limited by specific techniques and forms of a particular art in which every possible line of attack and defense is considered. It is also known as "styleless style."

Free-fighting technique is a combination of moves that react freely relative to the opponent's moves. For example, when an opponent moves back, you must be versatile, free from limitations and not bound to the specifications of any one technique or move during a real conflict. In *Tao of Jeet Kune Do*, Lee said, "When there is freedom from mechanical conditioning, there is simplicity."

Golden principle is the idea that each move must correspond with an opponent's. For example, if an opponent attacks, use a corresponding defense, like a stop-hit.

Hyperextension is the farthest a strike or kick can extend.

Interception is the essence of *jeet kune do*: Hit your opponent before he hits you. There are three ways to intercept: a block and hit, a simultaneous hit and block, or a hit followed by a block.

Independent movement does not telegraph or communicate preparation before an attack. It has no intention.

Lines of attack are lines along which an opponent can launch an attack. If kicking above the waist, the martial artist can attack along a high line. If kicking below the waist, the martial artist can attack along a low line. If punching above the elbow, the martial artist can attack along a high line, whereas below the elbow would involve a low-line attack. The inside line is the area inside the guard and centerline, while the outside line is outside the guard and centerline.

Movement time is the time it takes to perform one simple movement, whether it is a step forward or a kick.

Nonintention is a term Bruce Lee used to describe attacking without conscious thought. Consider it like this: When you launch an attack, it should be as if "it hit" rather than "you hit." By masking the preparation and hiding your intention, your opponent won't be able to guess your attack until after it lands. Like many things discussed in the book, this concept is very difficult to master but is what *jeet kune do* practitioners strive to achieve.

Pace, fraud, force are the three basic ways to attack. Pace means attacking with superior speed. Fraud involves deceiving an opponent by feinting or faking an attack to one line before switching to another. Force attacks remove a barrier by crashing into it.

Passive move describes what Bruce Lee considered the passive nature of many self-defense techniques. Because these techniques are based on blocking rather than hitting, they allow an adversary to take advantage of the time needed for the defender to block and then set up an attack. This means they lack nonintention (see "nonintention"), and Lee believed such moves lack efficiency. However, many *jeet kune do* moves are devised around taking advantage of an opponent who only blocks.

Point of vulnerability is when a *jeet kune do* practitioner is most at risk of being hit: during his attack, during his opponent's initial strike or during his follow-up. Be aware that attacking creates an opening for an opponent.

Reaction time is the time gap between a stimulus and a response. For example, reaction time occurs between an attacker's oncoming punch (the stimulus) and a defender's stop-hit (the response).

Relationship is the concept that you must move and react in relation to your opponent. In jeet kune do, this means a *jeet kune do* practitioner shouldn't attack an adversary based on pre-determined moves. Instead, he should attack based on how his opponent acts and reacts.

Renewed attack is the same attack performed twice on a particular opponent. For example, if a *jeet kune do* stylist launches a straight lead punch that is blocked, he quickly renews his attack on the same line. Use a renewed attack when an opponent retreats without adequate cover or if he stays and blocks. In boxing, this idea is known as "redoubling," and in fencing it is known as "*remise*."

Rhythm is a jeet kune do stylist's movement pattern during an attack.

Setup is using a series of attacks to create an opening for the final blow. For example, if you hit low with a straight punch and your opponent lowers his front arm to block it, you've set him up for a straight lead punch on a high line to the face.

Sensitivity refers to using touch rather than sight to react to an opponent. It is an important element in trapping hands. *Tai chi, hsing-i* and *wing chun* drills help students feel when an opening occurs or when an attack is blocked because relying on sight slows reaction time. Jeet kune do has borrowed and adapted some of these drills, but first-generation JKD students who are now teachers stick mostly with those from wing chun.

Single choice reaction is what a *jeet kune do* stylist strives to have. It means that when someone tries to hit him with a jab, he simply hits back first with a stop-hit. The stylist has one basic response to a single stimulus.

Stop-hit / stop-kick are considered the most efficient method of defense in *jeet kune do*. If an opponent tries to hit a JKD practitioner, the practitioner hits the opponent before the opponent's attack reaches the practitioner. Essentially, the JKD practitioner hits back with a stop-hit or stop-kick. Note: The stop-hit and stop-kick require great awareness and speed to pull off effectively.

Tempo is the one beat in a cadence that is the best time to accomplish the most effective action.

Time-commitment theory helps a *jeet kune do* stylist determine whether his attack or feint will be successful. To apply this theory and determine whether your chosen technique will work against a particular opponent, compare how much time it takes you to deliver the technique with how long it would take for your opponent to react and counter it. For example, the goal of a feint is to trick an opponent into blocking, which opens up a line for you to attack. Because blocking requires a greater time commitment than feinting, you can attack his opening before he has a chance to recover.